FOUNDATIONS OF
WINDOWS® NETWORKING

A MIRTHFUL (YET SURPRISINGLY-INFORMATIVE) INTRODUCTION

JOHN AUGUST SCHUMACHER

"Abandon all fear of acronyms, ye who enter here!"

Cover Art: "The Confusion of Tongues" by Gustave Doré, from *Doré's English Bible* (1866). Image from Wikimedia Commons (http://commons.wikimedia.org).

Cover design by John August Schumacher | Revised September 2013

http://www.johnaugustschumacher.com
http://www.goodreads.com/JohnAugustSchumacher

ISBN10: 978-1480238527
ISBN13: 148023852X

Published in the United States of America

TABLE OF CONTENTS

INTRODUCTION

First, An Analogy

When Alexander III of Macedonia ("Alexander the Great") established his ancient empire, he cultivated the Greek language and culture throughout the lands he had conquered. As a result, Greek became the *de facto* language of commerce for centuries to follow. Languages tend to simplify over time; the various Greek dialects had also been reduced in complexity over centuries of use. To wit: the Greek spoken in the marketplace was not the high Greek of Plato and Aristotle, but a new form called *Koinē* (koy ′nā), meaning "common."[1] One of Alexander's legacies was a foundation of common language by which business could be transacted throughout his empire.

Those who built the first iterations of what is now the Internet accomplished a similar feat, though for very different reasons. Alexander's first priority was not to spread Greek language, but to gain fame and fortune. Conversely, it was precisely the goal of a common language—that is, a set of communication standards by which computers would interact—that was foremost in the minds of those who connected machines into the first wide-area network. A similar intention lies behind the development of this study. By partaking, the reader will become familiar with the basic theory that underlies Windows computer networks, knowledge of which is necessary to troubleshoot and/or manage a network. At the same time, the reader is given a vocabulary of technical terms (including many acronyms!) that are the language of the trade.

The appendix includes links to specialized documentation that can provide additional information, *minutiae* that would only add to the bulk—but not the substance—of this

---

[1]Compare the Elizabethan English of Shakespeare to even the most eloquent of modern poetry and you will know the difference being alluded to here—to the great lament of philologists and linguaphiles everywhere. (That's scholars of ancient languages and "lovers of language," respectively, for those of you in Rio Linda.)

work. Diagrams and screenshots are my own, and are taken from a test instance of Windows Server 2008 R2. Please note that changes introduced with Windows Server 2012 put it outside the scope of this study. The fundamentals should remain the same, but the screenshots needed to show differences in the interface would have made this book unnecessarily cumbersome. URLs listed herein are live as of this writing (March 2013); a search engine query should suffice to find anything that is not accessible.

Dawn of the Internet Age

In the beginning, there was ARPANET, a project conducted by research universities and overseen by DARPA, the Defense Advanced Research Projects Agency. Several independent researchers had developed designs for a *packet-switching network*, a means by which communication could be sent and received over a single interface. Such a system would be *many-to-one* and *many-at-once*. Prior to that time, *circuit-switching* (e.g., the manual switchboard in the pre-computerized phone company) had been employed, which only allowed for point-to-point, one-at-a-time connection between parties. Packet-switching made possible the networking infrastructure on which the Internet would be built, with multiple end-points able to communicate with each other using virtual connections that could be created and removed as needed, apart from the underlying physical infrastructure.

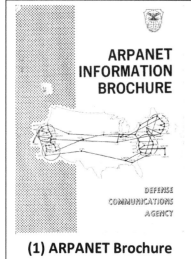

(1) ARPANET Brochure

The ability to do packet-switching with *virtual circuits* rather than *physical circuits* was a great leap forward. Another development was the adoption of a new protocol[2] called *TCP/IP*. This standard was to be "open" in the sense of not being tied to proprietary hardware; it could thus function across a variety of different physical equipment installations. Such a design made possible the idea of *internetworking*, linking disparate systems running different types of networking hardware (and, later, operating system software), but using the same hardware-agnostic protocols for communication. Along the way, the term *internet* was coined as shorthand for *internetworking*.

DARPA was instrumental in getting these new protocols adopted. As of January 1, 1983, TCP/IP became the only approved protocol

---

[2]A *protocol* is a set of rules about how information is exchanged between two parties, be they human beings or computers. (In the *Star Wars* series, C3PO was a "protocol droid ... fluent in over 6 million forms of communication.")

for the ever-growing ARPANET, a precursor to the modern Internet. In the meantime, a new type of network infrastructure was under development. Born of a joint venture between Digital, Intel, and Xerox in the 1970s, *Ethernet* would eventually surpass all rivals to become the *de facto* standard on which networks were built.

A Sidebar, If You Please...

Those familiar with mythology and philosophy will note that many of the terms used in computer networking are derived from ancient stories about gods and goddesses, mortals and monsters. *Aether* was the ancient Hellene[3] designation for the sky, space, or heaven. In ancient cosmology, however, *aether* also had metaphysical[4] properties, and was thought to be a substance that permeated all existence. The Stoics, a school of philosophy founded in Athens by Zeno of Citium in the 3rd century BCE,[5] believed that Nature or the universe was a living, reasoning substance composed of a passive agent (matter) and an active, intelligent agent that was described as a primordial fire. This active agent they called *Logos*, a Greek word with meanings ranging from "word" to "study" to "reason," and from which derives the English word *logic*. According to Stoic teaching, this *Logos* was the personification of Reason and Intelligence within creation.[6]

For the ancients, then, *aether* was not simply the "world above," but a living entity that imbued all creation with power and meaning. That this term should be used to describe communication between inanimate machines proves that those who built the foundations

---

[3]That's *Greeks* for those of you in Rio Linda. *Hellas* was the designation for what we English-speakers call the city-states that became Greece—hence the term *Hellenists* for those who promoted Greek language and culture (e.g., Alexander the Great, referenced earlier) and *Hellenized* for those so-influenced. (So no, this has nothing to do with where bad people go when they die. ☺)

[4]*Metaphysics* is that branch of philosophy that deals with "being as such"—the study of what it means "to be." For example, Plato famously taught that behind the physical world lies a realm of Forms or Ideas. There is thus a Form for a person, a dog, a tree, a color, etc. But more than just being a perfect version of a given thing, the Forms were for Plato the *essence of the thing itself*.

[5]*Before the Common Era*, a religiously-neutral term used in academic circles as a substitute for the Julian and Gregorian calendar designation *BC*, which means "Before Christ." Its counterpart is *Common Era* (CE), which replaces AD (*anno domini*), meaning "The Year of our Lord."

[6]The *Logos* was an instrumental part of Jewish and Christian thought in the centuries just before and after the Common Era. The Hellenistic (there's that word again!) Jewish philosopher Philo of Alexandria associated the *Logos* with Wisdom, which the Hebrew Bible had personified as an entity separate from the Godhead. In the New Testament, meanwhile, the *Gospel According to John* associated the *Logos* (which was said to be part of the Godhead itself) with Jesus of Nazareth. But we digress... (This is what you get for reading a technical manual written by someone with a master's degree in history and theology. ☺)

for the Internet were both well-educated and not without a sense of humor. On a more serious note, the concept is intriguing and the analogy apt. An *aether*-net is a medium common to all over which "words" (comprised of 0s and 1s) would be transmitted. The *aether*-net is also "intelligent," for it operates according to its own internal principles, much as nature has its own laws. (One hopes that the *aether*-net does not fulfill the Stoics' vision of primordial fire and thus scorch the servers, though this would be an interesting take on the science fiction narratives in which sentient computers cast off their human creators!)

But for such digressions, the words of the Spanish philosopher, Santayana, ring true:

> Those who cannot remember history are condemned to have it repeated to them by a scholar posing as a computer geek.[7]

We Now Return To Our Previously-Scheduled Topic…

In 1985, the Institute for Electrical and Electronic Engineers (IEEE, or "eye-triple-E") in the United States produced a standard called a *Request for Comment* (RFC) for *Local Area Networks* (LANs) bearing the catchy title "IEEE 802"—the 801 previous standards covering a broad range of topics from aeronautics to the national power grid. (A revision of the 802 standard, conveniently dubbed 802.3, later replaced the original specifications.)[8] The original 802 Ethernet specification ran at 10 Megabits-per-second (Mbps), but the 802.3 standard has now evolved to speeds up to 100 Gigabits-per-second (Gbps)![9] Each speed increase has maintained backward-compatibility, so a system running at 10Mbps or 100Mbps can interoperate with a server running at 1Gbps or even 10Gbps, given the appropriate hardware. In the original Ethernet configurations, a *repeater* (hub) was capable of only one speed. To connect hubs of different speeds together, a *bridge* was required. The bridge operated much like a transformer for electrical circuits, providing a means whereby the disparate speeds of the two networks could be linked. Ethernet *switches* have now merged both of these capabilities into one device. At a physical level, Ethernet was also designed to use a variety of different mediums (cable types), such as coax, copper, or

---

[7]OK, so perhaps this is not a direct quote. ☺

[8]Insomniacs, make note of this URL: http://standards.ieee.org!

[9]Another etymological aside is inevitable, as the proper pronunciation of *gigabit* has led some into considerable consternation (not to mention analytical alliteration. ☺) The consensus reached seems to be in favor of a hard *g*, as evidenced from http://en.wikipedia.org/wiki/Giga-. In *Back to the Future*, however, the learned doctor Emmet Brown pronounced it with a 'j' sound ("one point twenty-one jigawatts?!") Then again, one could ask: *Who really cares?*

fiber optic—or on no cabling at all, in the case of wireless (802.11 wireless Ethernet).

This introduction to Windows networking is intentionally limited to the Internet Protocol Version 4 (IPv4). It should be noted, however, that a newer protocol called IPv6 (IP Version 6) was incorporated into Windows starting with Vista. IPv6 was developed to overcome some of the limitations of IPv4, specifically, the number of address available for use. The two are quite different in practice, but the *theory* behind IP networking holds true for both, so what is learned with IPv4 translates into the world of IPv6.

This study is also limited to Ethernet, the *de facto* standard architecture for private (and even public) networks.[10] Those familiar with other materials (such as those published by Cisco Systems) may note that such favorites as Token Ring,[11] the Internetworking Packet Exchange (IPX),[12] and Frame Relay, are missing. These are simply beyond our scope, especially since modern LANs use TCP/IP over Ethernet.

The text is divided into sections that build upon one another, but can also be independently consulted as a reference. Chapter 1 opens with a high-level discussion of

---

[10]The term *private* is meant to connote a network that is owned and operated by a single entity (company or other organization). When such a network is limited to a single physical location, it is usually considered a Local Area Network (LAN). A Wide Area Network (WAN) is a collection of LANs that are separated physically and/or logically, i.e., owned by different entities, such as 2 companies or other organizations, each with their own private LAN. A WAN is *public* if, like the Internet, the entire infrastructure is not owned by any single entity. By contrast, a Metropolitan Area Network (MAN) designates a geographically-dispersed private network that extends a single LAN across multiple physical locations, but within the same geographical location, such as a city. An example of a MAN would be a large corporation with multiple offices spread across a given metro area that are connected together by physical (i.e., leased lines) or logical (i.e., point-to-point VPN) means.

[11]Token Ring was a competing (and, in some regards, superior) architecture to Ethernet that was popularized by IBM. The name derives from the "ring" architecture, in which all nodes were connected to a continuous loop of wire. Whereas Ethernet allows for all attached (nodes) to transmit simultaneously, Token Ring allowed only the node that held the token (as special type of data frame) to transmit. This reduced the broadcast traffic and allowed Token Ring to handle a higher percentage of overall traffic for a given amount of bandwidth.

A network is said to be *saturated* when all (or most) of its usable bandwidth is taken. When comparing 10Mbps Ethernet to 11Mbps Token Ring, Token Ring was the winner, for though they were nearly identical wire speeds, Token Ring offered a much higher saturation point. In the end, however, Ethernet won the popularity contest, especially after higher speeds (100Mbps, 1Gbps) were developed, which compensated for efficiency by offering raw bandwidth *capacity*.

[12]A proprietary protocol developed by Novell, IPX was popular during their reign as King of the Fileserver Market in the 80s and early 90s. IPX handled communication between workstations (which ran a Novell client program) and the backend fileservers, which ran the NetWare operating system. With the dawn of the Internet, it was not uncommon for IPX and IP to run on the same physical network, as users accessed their NetWare fileservers via IPX and other applications via IP. Over time, Novell versions of NetWare that could be operated with IP only.

the theory behind networking in general, and then details the OSI Model, the framework upon which IP networks are built. This is followed by discussions of network topology (Chapter 2) and design (Chapter 3). As such, Chapters 1-3 cover theory for Local Area Networks built on the IP protocol and Ethernet infrastructure.

Chapter 4 introduces terms and concepts specific to the world of Microsoft Windows. Chapter 5 then discusses the "behind-the-scenes" aspects of file and print sharing, while Chapter 6 delves into the computer browser service. Chapter 7, by far the longest section of the study, tackles Active Directory, including a quick look at administration tools. Chapter 7 also builds upon earlier discussion of the Domain Name System (DNS) as it relates to Active Directory. Chapter 8 provides an overview of Kerberos, the authentication protocol used by Active Directory in a Windows domain environment. Chapter 9 takes the reader through actual administrative tasks related to networking on a Windows system, with a focus on services such as DNS and DHCP. A series of appendices concludes the text, covering topics not directly applicable to the main text, but too involved for a simple footnote.

Finally, the bibliography and footnotes provide links to reference materials used in the preparation of this study, which the reader will find helpful for further study. Bear in mind that this introduction—though lengthy—is but a thumbnail sketch of a complex and multivalent topic. Myriad volumes have been produced about networking in general and the underpinnings of Windows in particular. Microsoft alone offers numerous whitepapers and other documents via the Support[13] and TechNet[14] sites. A full-length book on the principles of networking as related to the Windows operating system can be found in Joseph Davies' mammoth tome, *TCP/IP Fundamentals for Microsoft Windows*, available as a free eBook.[15]

---

[13]http://support.microsoft.com

[14]http://technet.microsoft.com/en-us/default.aspx

[15]http://www.microsoft.com/downloads/en/details.aspx?FamilyID=c76296fd-61c9-4079-a0bb-582bca4a846f&displaylang=en.

CHAPTER 1:
FANCY BOOK LEARNIN'
(THE THEORY OF NETWORKING)

In order to understand how a network functions, the following analogy is offered. Consider a house to which a street address has been assigned. This address is unique to that structure and cannot be changed. In order to communicate with others, a landline telephone is installed and assigned an identifier (phone number) that must be unique for that area code. Unlike the physical address, however, this telephone number *could* be changed or moved, and so is not tied to either this physical address or the phone itself.

In order to place a call, the user must know the number of the telephone to be reached. Conversely, the caller may only know the registered username or physical address with which that phone number is associated. This information is contained in the phone *directory* (to mirror the networking term), which cross-references the registered username to a particular phone number and the physical address where the telephone is installed.

+011	+1	(402)	867	5309
International Call Prefix	Country Code	Area Code	Branch/ Exchange	Subscriber Number

(2) Anatomy of a Phone Number

In the United States, a phone number is written as a sequence of digits (*country code*, *area code*, *exchange*, and *subscriber number*) prepended by a plus sign.[16] The country code is self-explanatory. An area code is assigned to a given

---

[16]The standard (E.164) behind this design was created by a specialized agency of the United Nations (UN) called the International Telecommunication Union (ITU). The specific division of the ITU responsible for the standard bears the lofty title *ITU Telecommunication Standardization Sector*

geographical space. (Large metropolitan areas may have multiple area codes.) The *exchange number* is associated with the *central office* by which it is interconnected to the remainder of the network. Finally, the *subscriber number* is a unique identifier for that particular phone on that exchange at that area code in that country. All told, the resulting string of digits produce a globally-unique telephone number.

In networking terminology, each country code, area code, or exchange number combination would be part of the *subnet*. Communication between area codes or subnets involves having traffic *routed* through an exchange (the Central Office in telephone terms, a *router* in networking terms) that is aware of all the subnets/area codes and can send information back and forth between them.

1.1
Method to the Madness: The OSI Reference Model

Before delving further into networking, a bit of theory is in order. Please refer to the diagram below. The information in this section will be referenced elsewhere to one degree or another, so familiarity with the concepts is helpful in understanding what is to come.

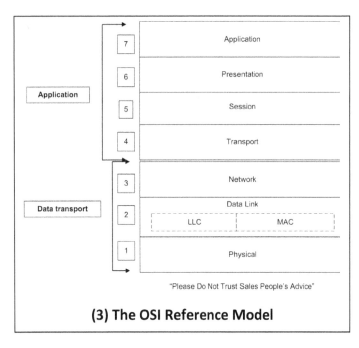

(3) The OSI Reference Model

The *Open System Interconnection (OSI) Reference Model* is a visual representation of how an application on one computer interacts or exchanges data with an application on another computer. It is comprised of seven layers, each of which has a specific purpose. Each layer, in turn, interacts with the layers "above" and "below" itself, as well as with its peer at the other end of a connection.

In order to help remember the OSI model, a mnemonic can be helpful. The most

---

(ITU-T). The E.164 standard defines international public telecommunications numbering plan used in Public Switched Telephone Networks (PSTN) around the world.

amusing one I have heard is this: "Please Do Not Trust Sales People's Advice."

1.1.1
"Peeling the Onion"

The first three layers of the OSI model are collectively known as the *Data Transport* layers. These are the physical/virtual foundation upon which the others are built. Within this grouping, the *Physical* and *Data Link* layers incorporate both hardware and software components. All other layers of the OSI Model are implemented in software only.

The OSI Model is based on the principle of *encapsulation*. To *encapsulate* an object is to place it within another object (for example, a capsule of pain reliever). In networking terms, encapsulation means information from upper-levels protocols are contained within lower-level *information units* called *packets* and *frames*. Data from the *Application* layer is encapsulated in the *Presentation* layer, and so forth. This data is then transmitted to the remote computer, where it is *decapsulated* and used. More on this will be said later.

1.1.1.1
Physical (Layer 1)

Our journey up the OSI stack starts at the *Physical* layer. As the name implies, this is the physical infrastructure (wiring, network devices, and related gadgets) on which the network operates. For our purposes, this is the Ethernet wiring (copper or fiber optic) used as a *medium* by which data is to be moved. The most common type of copper wiring used for Ethernet is *Unshielded Twisted Pair* (UTP). UTP cable consists of four pairs (8 wires total) that are twisted together and encased in a plastic sheathing.[17]

The idea of twisting wires together to compensate for *line noise*[18] was first conceived by Alexander Graham Bell. By arranging the wires in this fashion, Bell had discovered an easy way to solve the problem of *Electromagnetic Interference* (EMI). Twisted-pair cabling also reduces *crosstalk*, where the signal being transmitted on one circuit (wire) bleeds over to adjacent circuits and causes interference. For environments with high levels of EMI, UTP

---

[17]A word of warning to the adventurous: simply taking a spool of wire and fashioning a twisted pair cable of one's own will have mixed results. This is because the method by which the cable is produced is dictated by complicated mathematics. For example, the number of twists per length of wire (called the *pitch*) is only one part of the specification for a given type or (*category*) of cable. For more information on this topic, see Appendix C.

[18]*Line noise* commonly refers to interference (sometimes audible, such as on an analog telephone line) from external sources such as power lines, faulty connections, or damaged cabling.

cabling may not suffice. Instead, *Shielded Twisted Pair* (STP) cabling is used. The difference between the two is the sheathing used: UTP offers no electrical protection, while STP uses materials that are resistant to outside interference.

Alternately, Ethernet can be transmitted using specialized radio equipment as defined in RFCs 802.11b, 802.11g and 802.11n[19] and commonly called *Wifi*.

1.1.1.2
Data Link (Layer 2)

The *Data Link* is subdivided into the *Logical Link Control* (LLC) and *Media Access Control* (MAC) sub-layers. The MAC is associated with the physical address of a given node (device connected to the network), or more specifically, of the *Network Interface Card* (NIC) installed therein. Every node that will participate on an Ethernet network must have a NIC.[20] The NIC is the physical connection point between the device and the network, and is assigned a unique identifier called a *Media Access Control address*, or *MAC address*.

The LLC is concerned with *error control* and *flow control*. *Error control* is about managing the quality of the transmission, while *flow control* governs speed. This is something of a balancing act, for depending on the quality of the medium (wires or airwaves), quality of throughput (speed) may be affected by the error rate encountered. The NIC on Node A will only transmit as fast as it is able to reliably receive confirmation from the other Node B, so a number of factors come into play.[21] If the sending computer encounters errors

---

[19]802.11 is the number assigned to the original *Request for Comment* (RFC) published by the Institute of Electrical and Electronics Engineers (IEEE) which outlined the specifications for wireless Ethernet. Subsequent revisions have been published to reflect ever-increasing speeds available on wireless LANs: 802.11b operates at 11Mbps, 802.11g at 54Mbps, and 802.11n at 108Mbps, respectively. Information on the 802 standard, which incorporates both wired and wireless Ethernet, can be found here: http://standards.ieee.org/getieee802/index.html.

[20]In the past, it was common for the NIC to be an addon interface card for PCs or a PCMCIA (PC Card) or USB addon for laptops. This is no longer the case, as manufacturers commonly include a NIC that is integrated into the system board (a.k.a., *motherboard*) of the machine itself.

[21]Some common considerations are the relative speed of the hardware (CPU, memory, disk) involved. For example, a PC copying files to a server may be able to send files faster or slower than the receiving machine can handle, if the drive in the PC is relatively fast and the disk subsystem of the server is relatively slow or under heavy load.

For a physical connection (wired), the quality and speed of the NIC, wiring length and quality, number of network devices (*hops*) between the devices, and possible sources of EMI can affect the speed of the network. For wireless, the distance between the devices (if point-to-point) or from the wireless transceiver (if using a wireless access point), objects or materials that might block the radio signal. And, of course, there is always the load placed on the network by others!

(error control), it will adjust its transmission speed (flow control) up or down to ensure successful data transfer.

To help with flow control, the LLC allows for *multiplexing*, meaning the simultaneous transmission of multiple protocols across the same medium. For example, an Ethernet network can carry signals with multiple protocols, such as IP, IPX, NetBEUI, AppleTalk, and so forth. Each of these protocols is independent and separate from the others, but coexist on the network much as individual cars share a highway, each in their own lane.

The information unit at the Data Link layer is called a *frame*. A frame references its source and destination as a *Media Access Control* (MAC) address (more on this later). This information is contained in a *header*, the first of three fields (four counting the Preamble, discussed below) that comprise an *Ethernet frame*. Next comes the actual data (*encapsulated* from a higher layer in the OSI stack) being transmitted. Finally, a Data Link Layer *trailer*, which provides error correction in the form of a checksum value for the entire frame. When the recipient machine opens the frame, it compares this checksum value to the frame itself to see if the two match. If they do not, the frame is discarded. *Error-checking* ensures that what is advertised as the contents of the frame actually exists therein, and shows that those contents have not been altered or corrupted.

If all of this leaves you with a headache, take heart: the mechanics of Ethernet will be reviewed and explored in further detail in Section 1.3!

1.1.1.3
Network (Layer 3)

Layer 3 constitutes the *Network* layer, and provides routing capabilities by means of which 2 or more Data Link layers may communicate. For our purposes, two protocols operate at this layer. The first is the *Internet Control Message Protocol* (ICMP), which is utilized by the *ping* utility. The second is the *Router Information Protocol* (RIP). RIP shares information about different subnets between routers.[22]

The information unit at the Network layer (Layer 3) is the *packet*, composed of a *header* and *data payload*. This is encapsulated in the Layer 2 frame encountered above, and itself encapsulates higher-level protocols.

---

[22]Because of limitations associated with RIP, routers on the Internet use another protocol, the *Border Gateway Protocol* (BGP), which is better capable of handling the sheer scale of the task.

1.1.2
Recap: OSI Model Layers 1-3

As mentioned above, Layers 1-3 (Physical, Data Link, Network) of the OSI Reference Model are implemented in a combination of hardware and software. The following diagram visualizes the relationship between the three layers:a

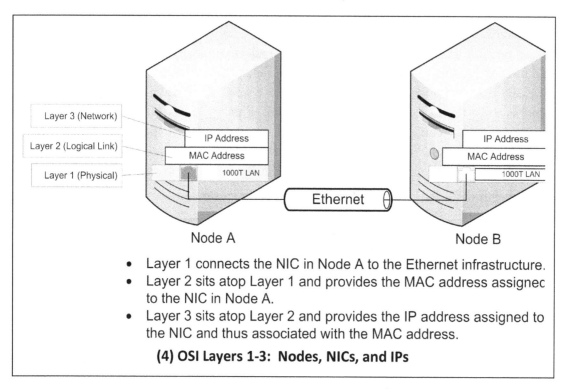

- Layer 1 connects the NIC in Node A to the Ethernet infrastructure.
- Layer 2 sits atop Layer 1 and provides the MAC address assigned to the NIC in Node A.
- Layer 3 sits atop Layer 2 and provides the IP address assigned to the NIC and thus associated with the MAC address.

(4) OSI Layers 1-3: Nodes, NICs, and IPs

1.1.2.1
Transport (Layer 4)

Layer 4 brings us to the Transport layer, charged with ensuring proper communication of data. It is here that the Transmission Control Protocol (the TCP in TCP/IP) resides, along with User Datagram Protocol (UDP) and Secure Session Layer (SSL). TCP provides error correction and delivery control for IP. UDP is "connectionless" and does not rely on the control mechanisms used by TCP. As a result, it can also perform faster for applications (like streaming video or audio) that can tolerate some loss in exchange for pure performance. SSL is a method of encryption used with TCP/IP applications such as the HyperText Transfer Protocol (HTTP), where the session itself (the virtual "tunnel" through which the data will pass) requires security.

1.1.2.2
Session (Layer 5)

Layer 5 of the OSI model is the Session layer. Functioning in an administrative role, the Session layer is responsible for creating, managing and terminating sessions (requests or responses) transmitted between applications running on separate nodes. For example, computer A is running a copy of a program that requests data from Computer B. It is the Session layer that interprets the request sent from Computer A to Computer B and then replies accordingly. The actual data sent is not handled by this layer, but it provides the mechanism by which the data exchange can take place.

1.1.2.3
Presentation (Layer 6)

Layer 6 is called the Presentation layer, and is where data encoding, formatting, and other "presentation"-related functions are accomplished. Compression and encryption are handled at Layer 6. This encryption differs from that at the Session layer (Layer 5) in that the Session layer provides a secure transport method, while the Presentation layer encrypts the actual data payload itself before it is sent. This allows the data to pass on an open network (unencrypted) but still be protected from unauthorized interception. Compression reduces the size of the data being sent by removing redundant bits (0s and 1s) without affecting the content per se. Thus, before the Application layer (Layer 7) is able to send any information out to another node on the network, that data must pass through Layer 6, where it is space-optimized and/or secured for its trip.

1.1.2.4
Application (Layer 7)

Finally, Layer 7 is the Application layer, the one closest to the applications running on a node. Such utilities as File Transfer Protocol (FTP), used for transferring files, or Simple Mail Transport Protocol (SMTP), used to send or receive email, operate at this layer. Again, when these protocols actually send any data, that information is handed off to the Presentation layer for processing, including compression and encryption. Likewise, when it reaches the other node, the information is not decrypted or decompressed until it rises up through the OSI stack and reaches Layer 6 on the remote machine. No other layer is aware of (or concerned with) the *contents* of the packet; they can only read the header.

1.1.3
Recap (or nightcap, if you prefer)

You have now traversed through the OSI model. You laid hands upon the Physical (Layer 1) and connected with the Data Link (Layer 2). You networked with Layer 3 (though the router was too busy to be much of a conversationalist). You have been beamed up by Scotty with the Transport layer (Layer 4) and been bored to tears by the Session layer (Layer 5). The Presentation layer (Layer 6) was all about appearances, but finally, at the Application layer (Layer 7), you could just kick back with a good game of Solitaire.

Before we turn attention to a more *ethereal* topic (so to speak), the foundation upon which all small networks (and many large ones) are based, the time is right for a crash course in network terminology.

Drum roll, please!

Ladies and gentlemen, I give you…the distinction between *bits* and *bytes*.

1.2
Love Bytes

A *bit* is the smallest unit of information used in a computer system, and corresponds to a single 1 or 0. A *byte* is comprised of 8 bits. Information is stored in bytes, but transmitted in bits. Thus, a hard drive is said to offer X number of bytes (or gigabytes or even terabytes, by today's standards) in size, while a network is measured in the number of bits it can transfer in a second. Because of the mathematics involved, a kilobyte (KB) is 1024 bytes, while a kilobit (Kb) is 1000 bits.[23]

When dealing with networking, the language changes to *bits per second* (bps). When dealing with multiples of bits (hundreds, thousands, millions), the same pattern, but rather than 1024, the multiplier is simply 1000.

---

[23]Technically, kilobyte should refer to 1000 bytes, while the enigmatic term *kibibyte* has been coined to mean the number 1024. A *kibibyte* is therefore 1024 bytes. In practical terms, I had never heard of this designation before doing research for this book, so it appears to be far from common parlance, even among those in the computer industry. (Quite frankly, it reminds me of a dog food commercial from a number of years back. Would a thousand bags of said product could be called Kibbles and Kibibits? ☺)

With all of this said, we get the following values:

Unit	Abbreviation	Value
1 byte	B	8 bits
1 kilobyte	KB	1024 bytes
1 megabyte	MB	1024KB
1 gigabyte	GB	1024MB
1 terabyte	TB	1024GB
1 kilobit	Kbits or Kb	1000 bits
1 megabit	Mbits or Mb	1000 Kb
1 gigabit	Gbits or Gb	1000 Mb

1.3
Pipes and Plumbing:
Ethernet Infrastructure Overview

As a *baseband* technology, Ethernet originally allowed only a single channel (signal) to traverse the physical *medium* (that's a fancy term for "wire"). *Baseband* is to be differentiated from *broadband* technologies whereby several signals can travel on the same physical medium. For example, the local cable company uses the same coax to provide a TV signal, telephone, and Internet. Likewise, the phone company offers DSL (Digital Subscriber Line) service that combines voice and data on the same wire. In fancy engineering terms, broadband is made possible through a technology called *multiplexing*, whereby different signals are transmitted over the same wire, either simultaneously or in tandem, and then interpreted and routed accordingly at the destination side of the circuit.

But we digress...

1.3.1
Don't Miss the Bus

The physical medium (wire or circuit board) that connects components within a computer, or multiple computers to each other, is called a *bus*. Simply put, a bus is an electrical circuit over which information is transmitted. A computer's innards contains a bus (wires or printed circuits on the system-board) that connects the memory, CPU and hard drive, as well as peripherals (locally-attached printers, etc.). Examples of an internal bus used for Intel-based computers would be ISA, EISA, AGP (used for video cards), PCI, and PCI Express. Examples of an external connection bus (for attaching peripherals or even other computers) would be the parallel port (used for older types of printers), RS-232 serial port (used for external modems), the Universal Serial Bus (USB), and FireWire.

1.3.2
The Evolution of Ethernet

Note that Ethernet is not listed here, because it is not itself a bus technology. An Ethernet Host Bus Adapter (HBA) is installed into an available slot within a machine, either as an add-on card or built into the system-board. The HBA then provides a connector for the cable used to connect this machine to the network. The earliest Ethernet networks used a single cable to connect 2 or more computers (called *nodes*) together. Because this cable was a thicker form of the coax used for cable television signals (CATV), it was nicknamed *thick net*. (Its official designation, 10Base5,[24] was less catchy.) Later, use of a smaller type of cable gave way to *thin net*, or the inauspicious 10Base2 standard. In either cases, coaxial cabling was strung as a loop or daisy-chain between nodes. As a result, it was called a *loop-bus topology*.

1.3.2.1
Please Indulge: An Etymological[25] Aside

The word *topology* derives from two Greek words: *topos*, meaning "place," and *logos*, meaning "word" or "study." Thus, a *topology* is literally "words [or pictures] about a place." In the field of mathematics, this has reference to the study of shapes that retain certain properties regardless of their shape, and is thus related to geometry. In computer science, a topology refers to the design of a network and the method by which the various participating devices (nodes) are interconnected. A *loop-bus* topology was the first such design. Since it formed a circle, the loop-bus was also known as the *ring topology*.

---

[24]The name is parsed as follows: "10" is the speed (10 megabits/second); "Base" refers to *baseband*; "5" refers to the maximum length of cable that can be used (100 meters, or ~1600 feet).

[25]That is, the study of a word's history. *Etymology* comes from the Greek *etymo* ("true") and *logos* ("word" or "reason" or "study")

1.3.3
The Ring and the Star (No...not *Ringo* Starr!)

The limitations of this *loop-bus* or *ring architecture* soon became clear. First, since all nodes were connected by a single loop of cable, a break anywhere in the connection caused problems for other nodes on the loop. Secondly, the logistics of stringing the loop itself were cumbersome, especially over long distances. The newer topology, still in use today, was to change the cabling from coax to a 4-pair type of wiring similar to that used for telephone systems. This cabling, called Unshielded Twisted Pair (UTP) was more flexible, of a smaller diameter, and more easily installed in walls or small spaces. UTP uses an RJ45 connector, the larger version of the RJ11 plug used with analog (and some digital) telephones.

Simply changing the cabling was an important step, but did nothing for the topology itself. That change, called *10BaseT* (with "T" referencing the use of UTP cabling, rather than coax) changed the actual method for establishing connections between nodes. Rather than a *bus* architecture, where a single loop connected all nodes, the 10BaseT model used a *star*, with a UTP cable from each node connecting back to a central device called a *hub*. The hub acted as a repeater, retransmitting transmissions from one computer to all others on the same hub. As a result, the star topology can also be called *hub-and-spoke*.

Whether using 10Base5, 10Base2, or 10BaseT cabling these first networks operated at speeds of 10Mbps (10 megabits per second). In time, 100BaseT (100 megabits per second,

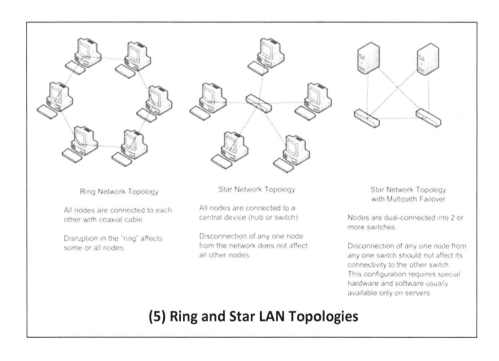

Ring Network Topology

All nodes are connected to each other with coaxial cable.

Disruption in the "ring" affects some or all nodes.

Star Network Topology

All nodes are connected to a central device (hub or switch).

Disconnection of any one node from the network does not affect all other nodes.

Star Network Topology with Multipath Failover

Nodes are dual-connected into 2 or more switches.

Disconnection of any one node from any one switch should not affect its connectivity to the other switch. This configuration requires special hardware and software usually available only on servers.

(5) Ring and Star LAN Topologies

or 100Mbps) networks were introduced, followed by 1000BaseT (1000 megabits per second, or 1Gbps, or simply "Gigabit").[26] Originally used for servers, gigabit is rapidly replacing 10/100 as the standard for workstations.

1.4
Calling All Stations: Ethernet At Work

Regardless of the physical topology or speed, Ethernet is a *broadcast* system whereby all nodes are free to transmit at any time.[27] A *broadcast* transmits data to all nodes on the network. By contrast, *unicast* transmissions are designed for one node only. Another form of transmission called *multicast* is also possible, and is used to transmit the same data to multiple nodes at once, but not all, as in the case of a broadcast. Broadcasts are used to accomplish various tasks, such as *discovery* of other nodes on the network. Unicast is then used for node-to-node communication. Multicast is used in streaming media (audio or video) situations, where the same content is delivered to multiple (intentionally-specified) nodes at once.

Because Ethernet supports broadcast, and since all nodes could transmit at once, the possibility exists for *collisions* to occur. A collision involves 2 or more nodes sending information out simultaneously and thereby conflicting with one another. In early networks, collisions were frequent, as no (easy) means existed to prevent them. What was developed, however, was a method of media-access called *Carrier-Sense Multiple Access/Collision Detection* (CSMA/CD). CSMA/CD instructs each node to first "listen" to the network to see if other nodes are transmitting. If nothing is detected after a specified time, the node is free to send its own data. However, because there is no rhyme or reason to this (2 or more nodes could, unknowingly to each other, be listening and then transmitting at the same time), a collision may still occur. In this case, both nodes cease transmitting for a set time (determined by an algorithm that assigns a random timeout period). When transmissions resume, it is assumed that both of these nodes will not retransmit at the same time again, though the possibility still exists that other nodes could then cause another collision, at which this whole process starts over, and continues until a node is able to transmit freely.

---

[26]The newest form of Ethernet, used for high speed "backbone" networks, is 10 *gigabits per second* (10Gbps). Conversely, the widely-advertised 3G/4G cellular networks are not, as the name implies, Gigabits-per-second, but considerably less: 14.4 Mbps downstream and 5.8 Mbps upstream at best, significantly slower than even a basic wired LAN can support.

[27]Ethernet is thus distinguished from other network systems, such as Token Ring, in which nodes are allowed to transmit only when in possession of a *token*.

Unlike early networks, collisions are rare on modern switched networks. This is because unlike the hub/repeater, a switch *segments* the nodes. A hub blindly retransmits each and every frame it receives to all attached nodes, a switch is more intelligent. Unlike a hub, a switch can read the header information of the frame as it passes through, and determine what node is the intended recipient. Moreover, nodes connected to a hub constitute a *broadcast domain*, where all nodes see the transmissions of all other nodes on that same segment.

By contrast, each port on a switch is its own broadcast domain, thus reducing or eliminating collisions, assuming that only one node is connected per switch port. (Collisions can still be a problem if the switch is connected to a hub, which then starts repeating all data it receives within that broadcast domain.) Furthermore, the broadcasts from any given node, attached as it is to a given switch port, only gets as far as the switch itself before it is examined and then sent only to the port on which the destination node has been detected.

1.4.1
"The Aim of a Frame Is To Put a Bracket Around Your Packet" (Say that 10 times fast)

As mentioned above, *frames* are information units at Layer 2, the Data Link layer, that encapsulate data from higher levels on the OSI stack. Much like an envelope can only hold so much, a frame is of a given size and contains a given amount of data. An Ethernet frame is typically 1500 bytes, as determined by the *Maximum Transmission Unit* (MTU), though some network devices are capable of handling *Jumbo frames* up to 9000 bytes. A frame smaller than 64 bytes is called a *runt*, and is discarded. (Runts are usually created by collisions.) A frame larger than 1518 bytes is called a *giant* and is also discarded. Giants are usually caused by *jabbering*, or a node that is transmitting in an non-standard way, indicating some sort of problem with the hardware—e.g., the PC's Network Interface Card (NIC), switch, or other network device.

Packets are information units at the Network layer, or Layer 3. The packet is a collection of data bits, to which the frame adds routing information needed to get it from sender to receiver. The distinction between frames and packets sometimes gets confused, and the terms used interchangeably. Technically speaking, a *frame* is a Layer 2 entity, while a *packet* is a Layer 3 entity. Furthermore, several different (though related) versions of Ethernet frames exist. The default configuration used by Windows is Ethernet II, though it can also send and receive the newer IEEE 802.3 standard. Because this discussion is focused on Windows, the following diagram displays the anatomy of an Ethernet II frame.

Details regarding the 802.3 and other standards is outside the scope of this study.

The *Datalink Header* is comprised of 4 parts. The first is the *Preamble*, a series of alternating 1s and 0s that announces the imminent arrival of a frame. This would throw all new meaning into the phrase "Framers" of the Constitution:

> We the nodes on the wire, in order to form a more perfect network, establish uptime, insure application reliability, provide for the common [malware] defense, promote user welfare, and secure the blessings of datagrams to ourselves and our posterity, do ordain and establish this Ethernet of the United Systems of the Internet.

But again, we digress...☺

Immediately following the Preamble is the *Destination Address*, a 6-byte (48 bits) field that corresponds to the 48-bit MAC address used by the network card of the intended recipient. This is followed by the *Source Address*, that is, the MAC address of the sender. The 2-byte (16 bits) *Ether type* field identifies the upper-level IP protocol being used (TCP, UDP). The *Data* field, 46-1500 bytes (368-12,000 bits) in length, is just what it is called: data received from an upper level protocol that is included in the frame for transfer across the physical network. (This process is called *encapsulation*, and will be addressed in the next section.)

Finally, the *Frame Check Sequence* (FCS) or Cyclic Redundancy Check (CRC) field provides for error correction. A CRC is a checksum generated based on the contents of the frame at the time that it is transmitted. Upon reception, the receiving node does its own CRC computation and compares the two values. If they do not match, a *CRC error* has occurred. This situation is caused by some problem with the transmission itself. Another type of error is a *misaligned* frame, in which the unit of bits encapsulated are less than 1 byte (8 bits). Again, this is caused by some issue on the physical medium, or from a problem when the frame was being formed in the first place. These two errors are often combined into a single designation of *CRC/Alignment error*, and represent a problem on the physical network itself. Possible issues include bad cabling, loose connection, or a problem with the NIC on one of the nodes.

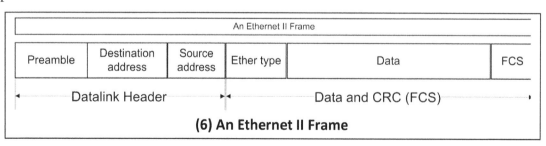

(6) An Ethernet II Frame

CRC and similar errors are difficult to diagnose without a view into the physical network, such as is possible with a *managed switch*. Windows will often not report the cause of the problem, because it is operating at a higher level of the OSI model, and thus cannot really understand what is going on. A managed switch, by contrast, has its own logs that see the frames as they enter and exit ports, and thus has a front-row seat into the Layer 2 operations of the network, where such errors actually occur. Unfortunately, managed or *intelligent* switches are still quite expensive, and thus not usually installed into a small network, so this tool is not available for troubleshooting needs that may arise.

1.4.2
'E' is for Encapsulate

In pharmacology, a *capsule* is a dissolvable tube containing a substance of medicinal value. Likewise, a *space capsule* is a compartment in which astronauts are placed for their journey to the stars. In networking terms, the capsule is one data unit (such as an Ethernet frame) that contains within it another type of data unit, such as an IP packet). The IP packet (a Layer 3 entity) is therefore *encapsulated* in the frame (a Layer-2 entity) for transport. The diagram on the following page visualizes this concept.

Like the Ethernet frame in which it is contained, the IPv4 packet (also called a *datagram*) is comprised of a header and data sections. The header is divided into 12 fields or subunits, each of which have a specific purpose. Starting at the top of the diagram, the first field is the 4-bit *Version*, which indicates the version of IP being used (e.g., IPv4 vs. IPv6). For our purposes, this will always be IPv4.

Next is the 4-bit *Internet Header Length* (IHL), which gives the length of the IP header in 32-bit "words." Each "word" accounts for a certain amount of length of the IP header itself. The IHL is important because an IPv4 header is not a fixed length (like an Ethernet frame header) and can contain various options. The minimum value for this field is 5. If each "word" is 32-bits, then the minimum size of the header is 5 x 32, or 160 bits (20 bytes). The maximum value is 15 words, or 15 x 32 480 bits (60 bytes).

The *Differentiated Services* (abbreviated *DiffServ*) field allows for specific settings related to certain upper-level protocols. An example of this is the specific requirements around Voice-Over-IP (VoIP). The *Total Length* field (which is unfortunately not abbreviated *TotLen*) denotes the length in bytes of the entire IP packet, including the header and data payload. *Identification* is a marker identifying the current datagram, and is used in the case of fragmentation, in order to reassemble the datagrams correctly.

The next field on the diagram, *Flags*, contains 3 bits. The first (*Bit0*) is reserved. The second and third specify two things: (1) whether or not the packet can be fragmented, and if so, (2) whether it is the last in a series of fragmented packets. Using the table below, we see that if *Bit1* is set to zero, the datagram may be fragmented. Likewise, if *Bit2* is set to 1, additional fragments are yet to be received. The following table shows the bit values and meanings:

Value	Bit0*	Bit1	Bit2
0	0	May	Last
1	0	Do Not	More
*Bit0 is reserved and always value '0'			

The process is detailed in the following diagram.

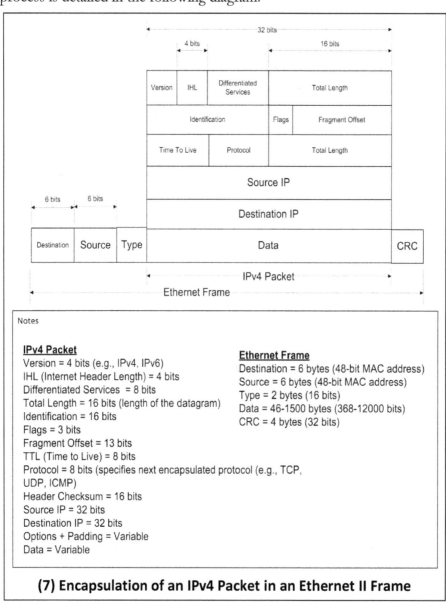

(7) Encapsulation of an IPv4 Packet in an Ethernet II Frame

1.4.3
Data Fragmentation

The *Maximum Transmission Unit* (MTU) is associated with the Data Link and Network layers (Layers 2 and 3) of the OSI Model, and has reference to the maximum size a single data unit can be in order to be sent as a whole. The default MTU used by Ethernet II and across the Internet is 1500 bytes.[28] *IP Datagram Fragmentation* refers to the process by which a datagram larger than the MTU is divided into pieces which are transmitted separately and then reassembled by the receiver node.

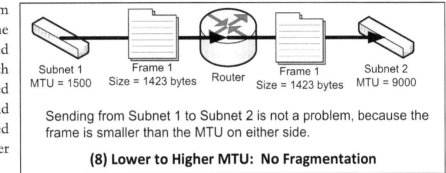

Subnet 1
MTU = 1500

Frame 1
Size = 1423 bytes

Router

Frame 1
Size = 1423 bytes

Subnet 2
MTU = 9000

Sending from Subnet 1 to Subnet 2 is not a problem, because the frame is smaller than the MTU on either side.

(8) Lower to Higher MTU: No Fragmentation

The *Fragment Offset* indicates the position of the data within the fragment relative to its position in the original datagram. This allows the destination node's IP protocol stack to properly reconstruct the whole datagram from the fragments.

Fragmentation can cause delays and performance issues on the network, because any fragment not received correctly by the recipient requires that *all* fragments be retransmitted. Thus, if a non-standard MTU is intended, it should be end-to-end, to avoid any fragmentation of the datagrams as they travel across the network. This means that all network devices along the path must support the non-standard or *Jumbo* frames.

The same is not the case in the reverse, however. When a frame is generated from the network that allows jumbo frames, it is given the maximum allowable payload of 9000 bytes. This enters the router and is to be processed accordingly, but before it can traverse to the other side, the issue of frame size must be addressed. In short, the MTU of the destination network is 6 times smaller than the sender. The frame must therefore be divided up (*fragmented*) into units small enough to fit the MTU of Subnet 1.

---

[28]Specialized networks, such as dedicated backup LANs or other high-throughput segments, may utilize an MTU much higher than the default 1500 setting. For example, most enterprise switches support "Jumbo frames" with an MTU of up to 9000. The result is that more information is sent per-packet, with a corresponding increase in network efficiency and performance. The trade-off, however, is that *all* NICs attached to the segment, as well as the switches, routers, and other devices (and their operating systems) must be compatible with this larger MTU and be configured accordingly.

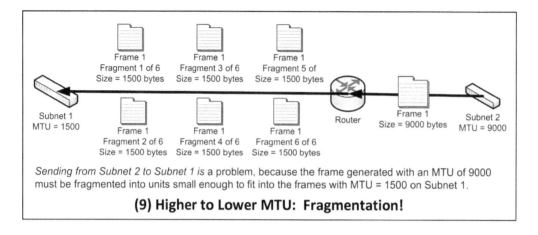

Sending from Subnet 2 to Subnet 1 *is* a problem, because the frame generated with an MTU of 9000 must be fragmented into units small enough to fit into the frames with MTU = 1500 on Subnet 1.

(9) Higher to Lower MTU: Fragmentation!

This begs another question: *can* the frames be fragmented? In terms of the discussion above, the answer depends on whether the 2nd bit (*Bit1*) in the *Flags* field is set to 0 (*allow*) or 1 (*disallow*). Here again is the chart, for easy reference:

Value	Bit0*	Bit1	Bit2
0	0	May	Last
1	0	Do Not	More
*Bit0 is reserved and always value '0'			

Assuming that the flag is set to 0 for "allow" the router proceeds with the work of fragmentation; if it is set to 1 for "disallow" fragmentation is not allowed, and the frame will be discarded). The single frame sent from Subnet 2 is thus broken into 6 pieces, each of which bear a designation that they are fragments of the original. The 3rd bit (*Bit2* in the chart above) in the *Flags* field is therefore set to 0 for the first five of these fragments, and to 1 for the sixth. When the frames reach the receiving node, it knows first of all that the frame has been fragmented, and secondly, which is the last in the series. Using the information in the *Identification* and *Fragment Offset* fields, the receiving node can then reassemble the fragments into its original frame, which is processed in the OSI stack.

But yet again, we digress.[29]

---

[29]I do apologize, as this seems to be a pattern. Those responsible have been locked in the server room. ☺

1.4.4
TTL: A Time to Live, A Time to Die

Returning to our discussion of the IP Header, we come to Time-to-Live (TTL), a counter that decrements (decreases) by 1 each time the packet is handled by a router or switch. These points of contact, called *hops*, are the virtual stepping-stones by which the frame makes its way from Point A to Point B. If the TTL reaches zero before reaching its destination, it is discarded at the next hop. This methodology was designed to keep itinerate datagrams from endlessly circumnavigating the Internet, thus becoming a LAN without a country.[30]

Next on the menu is the *Protocol* field, which offers a preview of the upper-layer protocol that will receive the packets after being processed by the IP stack. The *Header Checksum* provides a means of ensuring that IP header integrity. The *Source* and *Destination IPs* are self-explanatory, and so we come at last to the *Data*—that is, the payload destined for another layer of the OSI Model. Just as the IP datagram or packet is encapsulated inside the Ethernet II Frame, so also the payload (data using the TCP or UDP protocol) is encapsulated inside the IP packet.

And now for something completely different...

1.5
Sitting On A Cloud

In the previous sections, we contemplated the structure of all that was to come: the OSI model. We then considered some of the foundational terminology that is to be built upon later, and took a glimpse behind the curtain, to get the first look at the inner-workings of Ethernet. We now step away from the curtain and, having ascended Mt. Olympus, sip of the ethereal nectar that the digital gods would have us drink, while reclining beneath the Tree of Knowledge.[31] Such a vantage point among the mountain peaks gives us a good place from which to segue to our next topic...wait for it..."The Cloud."

[Cue the sound effects]

---

[30]OK, bad pun *and* technically incorrect...but I bet it made you smile. ☺

[31]Or, alternatively, pour some vodka over ice, down some aspirin, and hope it is all just a bad dream from which we will shortly awaken.

"The Cloud" is a term used to describe the rather nebulous makeup of the Internet, which is itself nothing but a collection of smaller networks. In order to understand the (virtual) terrain, it is important to get our bearings. Attaching a computer to the Internet has been made easy these days, due to the proliferation of cheap and available bandwidth and the (relative) simplicity of modern "Plug-and-Play" computers.[32] How this all works will be the subject of Chapter 2, in which the details of network topology will be explored. For now, it is important to shed light on the organization of the Internet from a logical perspective.

1.5.1
The Network Address Space

In a previous section, we introduced the analogy of a house, into which a land-line telephone has been installed. Both the house and the phone have unique identifiers, similar to the MAC and IP of a network-attached computer. What is unknown is the pattern, if any, that is followed in making these assignments. This brings us to the issue of *address space*, or again...wait for it...*wait* for it..."The Cloud."

Addresses for public IPv4 are arranged into three *classes*, called (conveniently enough) Class A, Class B, and Class C. Two additional classes (D and E), are reserved for non-public use.[33] The class of network addresses used determines the maximum number of hosts that can be included in that network. For example, a Class C network using IP version 4 (IPv4) can have a maximum of 2547. hosts.[34] Each group of hosts is called a *segment* or *subnet* (the distinction between these terms will be discussed later).

---

[32]Or is it "plug-and-*pray*?"

[33]These designations were originally made by the Internet Assigned Numbers Authority (IANA), an outgrowth of DARPA, one of the entities that formed the network that became the Internet. Since the 1990s, however, this function has been given to a non-profit corporation called the Internet Corporation for Assigned Names and Numbers (ICANN),which operates under a contract from the U.S. Department of Commerce.

[34]To overcome the limitations of the 32-bit IPv4 network classes, IP version 6 (IPv6) was created as a new method of assigning addresses. IPv6 uses a 128-bit address (vs. 32-bits for IPv4), and thus has a exponentially –greater range of available addresses: about 3.4×10^{38} total! Due to the scope of this study, the information here deals only with IPv4.

1.6
What's In a Name?

Machines are perfectly content to identify themselves with long strings of numbers, but we humans prefer names. Having anthropomorphized our gadgets, we insist upon giving them names them as well. This is not without a pragmatic side, of course. Suppose that a NIC with MAC address 00:21:6B:52:8C:CA is installed into a node that is then assigned IP address 192.168.1.100 and hostname "Laptop." (Which of these designations is easiest for *you* to remember?) Despite such efforts at domestication, however, machines will continue to using the 0s and 1s to identify themselves and others on the network. How, then can a human reference "Laptop" when trying to connect to this machine, rather than having to remember the numbers?

1.6.1
The HOSTS File

In order to track the names and number assigned to different computers on a network, some method of cross-reference or *name resolution* is necessary. The first solution devised was to have a HOSTS file, a simple text file that lists IP addresses and their respective hostnames. A hash symbol (#) placed in front of a line indicates a comment that is ignored when the file is parsed by the system.[35]

A HOSTS file functions as a rudimentary tool for lookups, but is somewhat clumsy. For starters, this file must be copied to each node on the network. Any subsequent changes to the information contained in the HOSTS file must then be updated on *each* node. For small networks that are relatively static (that is, on which machines configurations are not often added or changed), this works fine; on larger networks, however, it quickly becomes untenable.

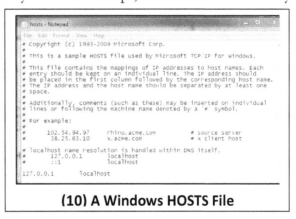

(10) A Windows HOSTS File

---

[35]This is similar to the "REM" command in MS-DOS batch files.

1.7
The Domain Name Space

The solution reached in the early days of the Internet was two-fold. First, hosts were to be organized into *domains*, with different designations by broad category. These designations, such as the familiar *.com*, were appended to the domain name, and were called, cleverly enough, *Top Level Domains* (TLDs). Say that domain *xyz.com* is the public name space for XYZ Corporation, which is part of the larger group of domains intended for commercial enterprises (*.com*). Domains are hierarchical, with each level separated by dots, and the top level (or *root*) designated by a single dot. In the 1980s, seven *Generic Top Level Domains* (gTLDs) were created. Unrestricted registrations allowed within three of these (*.com*, *.net*, and *.org*); the remaining 4 were reserved for specific purposes. Since that time, a number of other TLDs (for example, *.biz* or *.info*), have been created for various purposes. Finally, *Country Code Top-Level Domains* (ccTLDs) are used for a given country or dependent territory. Some of these country codes are easily recognized, such as *.uk* for the United Kingdom, or *.tw* for Taiwan, while others are less obvious, such as *.ch* for Switzerland.[36]

The following diagram shows some of the top level domain designations:

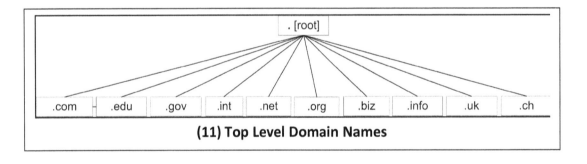

(11) Top Level Domain Names

---

[36]The *CH* is derived from the Latin *Confederatio Helvetica* ("Helvetic Confederation") the name given to the central government established under the Swiss Federal Constitution in 1848. (See what happens when you put an historian in charge of network documentation?!)

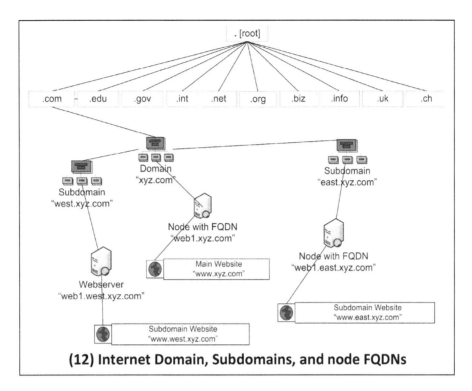

(12) Internet Domain, Subdomains, and node FQDNs

1.7.1
Fully Qualified Domain Names

When a particular hostname is prepended to this domain name, we have what is referred to as a *Fully Qualified Domain Name* (FQDN). This is to be distinguished from a *Uniform Resource Locator* (URL), insofar as a URL points to an Internet site or service, while an FQDN points to a given node on a network. Thus, *xyz.com* is a domain name, *www.xyz.com* is a web property, and *web1.xyz.com* would be the FQDN of a specific node within that domain.[37]

Fully-Qualified Domain Names become especially important when the domain itself is divided according to some hierarchy. A domain that exists as part of (or *under*) another domain is called a *subdomain*. Subdomains are often used to give logical names to geographically-dispersed resources. For example, let us say that XYZ Corporation has two divisions, called simply East and West. Each of these could be included into same domain (xyz.com), but the decision was made that each is to be treated as a semi-autonomous

---

[37]Technically, an FQDN ends with a dot, indicating the root of the domain name space. In common usage, however, this syntax is often ignored and the trailing dot simply left off. The exception is a configuration files that reference a FQDN and may not understand the entry if it does not follow the proper syntax, ending dot included.

business unit, with appropriate identity both internally and externally. Thus, 2 subdomains called *east.xyz.com* and *west.xyz.com*, respectively, each maintain their own web properties or services. Extending the diagram from the previous section, we see that under the *.com* domain there exists a domain called *xyz.com*. The main web site on this domain is called *www.xyz.com*. The server hosting this site has a hostname of *web1*; hence, its FQDN is *web1.xyz.com*. In addition, *xyz.com* has been divided into sub-domains, each of which has its own website.

1.7.2
DNS: The Domain Name Service

As mentioned above, the HOSTS file can be used to resolve hostnames (including Fully Qualify Domain Names) to IP addresses. The HOSTS is thus like a published phone book. As long as the information contained therein is comports with reality (i.e., changes are not made that are not reflected until a newer edition is published), all is well. Since organizations and individuals tend to keep the same phone number and address, this works reasonable well. Given the rapid growth of the Internet, however, combined with the sheer numbers of hosts and/or addresses to be included, the same is not the case with computers, and the HOSTS solution was deemed untenable. The solution to this problem was to introduce a virtual directory that would provide a means of resolving domain names to IP addresses. The *Domain Name Service* (DNS) is a program running on a *name server* and managing the directory of hostnames and IP addresses for a group of computers. DNS is divided into *zones*, groupings that correspond to the domain for which they are active. This information is then *propagated* between different name servers in order to keep the directory updated across systems or locations.

Like the Domain Name Space which it serves, DNS is arranged as a hierarchy or "tree," with a number of name servers at the top (or *root*) of the hierarchy. So-called *Root Name Servers* contain information for all Top-Level Domains (TLDs). These machines are managed by various organizations at the behest of the DNS Root Server System Advisory Committee, one of several committees that are part of the Internet Corporation for Assigned Names and Numbers (ICANN). Root DNS servers bear host- and domain names that follow the schema *letter.root-servers.net*, where *letter* ranges from A through M.[38] There are thus 13 root domain name servers that hold DNS information for all of the TLDs, with FQDNs of *a.root-servers.net*, *b.root-servers.net*, and so forth.

---

[38] As presented to the world, a given root name server appears to be a single entity, i.e., *a* server hosting DNS. In reality, root name servers are clusters of machines configured for redundancy. This complexity is hidden from view to the outside, but allows for DNS to be highly-available.

From the root of the DNS tree extends various offshoots called *leaves*, corresponding to the various root domains (TLDs). Each leaf contain *resourced records* that hold information about that domain. The DNS tree is also divided into *zones*, at the top of which is the *root zone*. Zone information (the resource records mentioned above) is stored in a database on name server. A name server that contains zone information for a given domain is considered to be *authoritative* for that domain. Thus, the root servers are authoritative for the TLDs, for they contain the zone information for the Top-Level Domains (*.com*, *.net*, and so forth). However, because administration of the myriad domains that exist on the Internet would be unfeasible, root servers do not contain all of this information. Rather, through a process of *delegation*, a portion of the zone (corresponding to a given domain or sub-domain) is given to another, separate domain name server. This second-tier DNS server then becomes *authoritative* for that domain (and its sub-domains, if applicable). At least one, but more often 2 or more for redundancy, authoritative DNS server(s) must be configured for a given domain. More on DNS will follow in the section on Active Directory, which uses DNS for its own operations.

Note from the diagram below that the root domain *xyz.com* and both sub-domains have their own DNS, file server, email server, and web server. This is a somewhat extreme example, but is meant to show the logical layout of such an organization. The DNS server under the root domain (xyz.com) would be *authoritative* for that domain. Thus, its zone would include resource records for the nodes within that sub-domain. The DNS server in each sub-domain would likewise contain a zone with resource records for that sub-domain.

1.8
Q&A: DNS Query and Response

How then does a workstation at XYZ access this information? For example, when the email client (e.g., Outlook) is opened, the workstation must know how to reach the email server across the network. In order to do so, it needs to know the IP address (and MAC) of the server in question. The user does not have access to this information (and would not want the hassle). Instead, the operating system of the workstation will execute a background function called a *DNS query*. In Windows, this command is called *nslookup*. The query is performed against whatever DNS server has been configured as part of the TCP/IP configuration on the machine. If that server does not know the answer, it will send the request up to a different DNS server. The DNS server to which the request is sent is based on a record called a *forwarder*, which is stored in the configuration of the DNS server, and is comprised of a list of public DNS servers (usually as maintained by the ISP to which the server is connected).

The process of forwarding DNS requests automatically from server to server is called *recursion*. If configured to support recursion, each DNS server will continue to forward the request until it receives an answer from an authoritative DNS server higher up the chain.

The process works as follows:

1. A user points a web browser to www.xyz.com.
2. The client PC does not know the IP address for this website, and so queries (shown in red) a DNS server managed by its ISP: "Where (i.e., at what IP) is www.xyz.com?"
3. The ISP-managed DNS server does not know the answer, since it is not an authoritative name server for that domain. What it does know is the IP of a root server that can identify the DNS server that is authoritative for domain xyz.com.
4. The ISP-managed DNS server queries this root name server to ask for the IP address of the authoritative DNS server for domain xyz.com
5. The root DNS server responds that the authoritative DNS server for domain xyz.com is at IP address 3.3.3.3.
6. With this information, the ISP-managed DNS server issues a query to the public DNS server (ns1.isp.com) that is authoritative for domain xyz.com, asking for the IP address of the website called www.xyz.com.
7. The authoritative DNS server ns1.xyz.com responds that www.xyz.com is at IP 1.2.3.4. The ISP-managed DNS server sends this on to the client PC.
8. The client PC is now able to connect to the website by issuing a GET command from the browser to call up the main page at www.xyz.com.
9. The web server hosting this site responds (shown in purple) with the landing page for the xyz.com website, in effect stating in reply: "Welcome to www.xyz.com."

As described above, all of this is completely transparent not only to the end-user, but to the client PC itself, for the DNS server to which it issued its original query handled the task of finding the appropriate information from the other DNS servers, using the *recursion* process described above. Consider the following diagram:

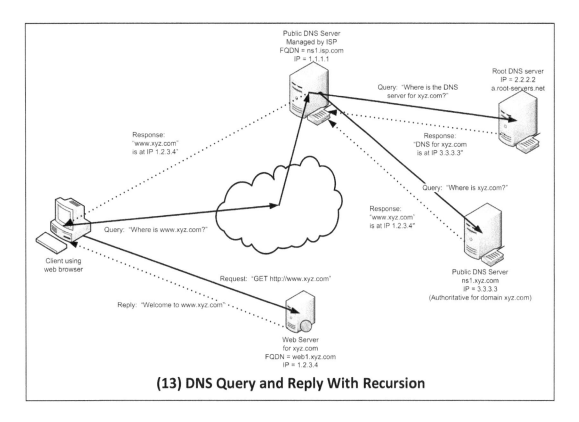

(13) DNS Query and Reply With Recursion

1.8.1
Reverse DNS Query (RDNS)

The same process of querying a DNS server for information about a host can be done in reverse. In this case, the IP address is known, but the hostname is not. The query thus specifies an IP and receives in reply the hostname (if known) that is assigned to that IP.

1.8.2
Cold Hard Cache

The client PC is now connected to the website it requested. What, however, if this browser session is closed and then reopened later? Does the entire process need to take place again? The answer is (or should be) no. The reason for this is that *caching* should be taking place at one or more places along the way. A *cache*[39] is a section of virtual or physical memory (RAM or disk) on the computer that holds a copy of what has been done or seen before. Thus, for every site that is visited, the resulting page(s) are cached in the

---

[39]The English word *cache* comes from the French *cacher* ("to hide").

browser, unless otherwise configured. This allows websites that are not frequently changed to load more quickly when visited again and again: the Internet speed remains the same, but rather than retrieve the content from the web server, the page is loaded locally from cache.

The same concept applies to DNS. A cache of known hostnames or web addresses and their corresponding IP addresses is stored in cache. Actually, on a given machine, there may be more than one cache: one in the browser itself, another in the operating system, and yet another on the DNS server(s) that it queries. This situation has both positive and negative consequences. Assuming the information is accurate, it allows a computer to find the resource for which it is looking that much faster. After all, even though the recursion query process described above is quick, having a local copy of the data readily accessible is always *faster*. However, if this information is outdated or simply wrong, the cache can be a detriment, insofar as the browser or operating system will continue to use this incorrect information and never find its destination.

To belay this situation, the cache is usually configured with a timeout function (similar to the Time-to-Live described for Ethernet frames). "Stale" records are then discarded, and a DNS query issued to update the cache. A similar principle is used between DNS servers. For example, an office may have a local Windows server configured for DNS (which is required for a Windows domain). By default, this Windows DNS service will cache the responses it receives to queries that it forwards out to public name servers. Thus, if the user at this office accesses the website for xyz.com, the local Windows server (in addition to the browser and operating system of the PC) "remembers" the information and can respond accordingly next time a query is received. This is known as a *non-authoritative* response, for the server does not have zone information for that domain in its own DNS configuration; instead, it is relying on a cache of the response received from another DNS server elsewhere.

Understanding how the DNS cache works is helpful in troubleshooting issues that may arise when a user is no longer able to connect to a site or resource that is known to be available to others. By clearing the cache at the browser, operating system, or even DNS server level, the issue may be resolved. The system is then forced to query an outside (authoritative) server via the recursion process described above, and will (hopefully) get the correct an answer.

CHAPTER 2:
NETWORK TOPOLOGY

2.1
Getting Your (Virtual) Bearings

As mentioned above, a *topology* is a map. A network topology is thus a map of the network, viewed either from a physical (devices, wiring, and blinking lights) or logical (i.e., how those devices function or interact) perspective. The following discussion builds upon the theory outlined in Chapter 1 of this study. As discussed, Layers 1-3 of the OSI Reference Model correspond to physical and logical entities within an Ethernet network. Delving into this realm, we will now examine each of these in turn, starting with the foundation: the Physical layer.

2.2
Nodes and NICs (Layer 1/Physical Layer)

The foundation of any network is the physical hardware—that is the devices and the wiring that interconnects them. In networking terminology, a computer or other device (e.g., printer or appliance) attached to a network is called a *node*. Technically, 2 or more nodes are required to constitute a network. When located together, either physically or logically, the result is called a Local Area Network (LAN). When geographically dispersed, it is called a Wide Area Network (WAN).

For a node to communicate on the network, it must have a Network Interface Card (NIC). In the world of Ethernet, this can be wired or wireless, integrated or add-on. An integrated NIC is part of the system itself, and is usually a chipset soldered onto the system-board. As such, it is not easily (if at all) replaceable, but may be enabled or disabled via software. An add-on NIC for a desktop PC could be installed into an internal expansion slot, or connected to a USB slot. On a laptop, the add-on NIC is either a USB device or a card that installs into the PCMCIA (also called a PC Card) or CardSlot on the side of the machine.

In most circumstances, a wired Ethernet interface uses an RJ45 jack, the larger version of the RJ11 connector used in telephone systems. This is then connected to the network (hub, switch, or elsewhere) with a Category 5 (Cat5) or Category 6 (Cat6) Unshielded Twisted Pair (UTP) cable. Cat5 cabling is common in small networks, as it supports speeds up to 100Mbps. Nodes connecting with the faster Gigabit (1000Mbps) speed need a Cat5e (for Enhanced) or Cat6 cable in order to function properly, as Cat5 does not support Gigabit speeds. Servers, switches, and certain other high-end equipment sometimes use fiber optic NICs and cabling, which transmits data via laser beam. Finally, with the advent of 10 gigabit Ethernet (10GE), still another type of connector was introduced: the 10BaseG-CX4.

2.3
"Hey, MAC, you got an address?"
(Layer 2/Data Link Layer)

When a NIC is manufactured, it is programmed with a unique identifier called a *MAC address*. We've seen the MAC or *Media Access Control* above, as one of the sub-layers of the Data Link layer on the OSI Model. The MAC Address is also called a *burned-in address*, for its information is written (*burned*) onto a *Read-Only Memory* (ROM) chip by the manufacturer.

A MAC address is a 48-bit hexadecimal (hex) string, comprised of two 24-bit segments. The string is sometimes written together, but for sake of legibility (i.e., to make it more human readable), may be separated by colons or dashes:

00216B528CCA	Computer readable
00-21-6B-52-8C-CA	Human readable example 1
00:21:6B:52:8C:CA	Human readable example 2
00216B-528CCA	Human readable example 3

The first six octets identify the manufacturer, while the remaining 6 octets are a serial number or other unique identifier. Taken together, these are intended to be unique world-wide, and cannot be changed.[40] By using a 48-bit address space, there are potentially 2^{48} or 281,474,976,710,656 maximum unique MAC addresses available. Assuming a world population of ~6 billion people, that would provide MAC addresses to 46,912 network-attached gadgets for every man, woman, and child on Earth!

2.3.1
The Address Resolution Protocol (Layer 2/Link Layer)

Nodes on a network communicate with each other by MAC address. Higher layers of the OSI model, however, use the IP address to identify a given remote node. In order to "translate" between these two addresses, a node uses the *Address Resolution Protocol* (ARP). ARP maintains a cache of known MAC addresses and IP addresses.

In the example, the application running on PC1 communicates with an application running on PC2. PC1 knows that the application can be found at IP address 192.168.1.101. The request is thus generated in the application (layer 7 of the OSI model) and then passed down through the layers until it reaches Layer 2. At Layer 2, ARP determines that the IP address for PC2 is not located in the local ARP cache. It therefore issues an ARP request with a query, "Who has IP 192.168.1.101"—that is to say, "To what NIC is this IP address assigned, and what is the MAC address of that NIC?"

In this example, both PCs are connected to a switch, which maintains its own ARP cache tables. Though not shown in the simplified diagram below, the switch would also be sending and receiving ARP requests and replies from the nodes that are connected to it.

Thus, a switch is able to "learn" the MAC addresses of the nodes connected to it.

---

[40]It is not possible to change the MAC assigned to a NIC, since that information is burned into the adapter hardware itself. It is, however, possible to present a different MAC to the network, via special software. Advanced configurations involving servers with multiple NICs that are "trunked" or "bonded" together to form a single, larger connection use specialized software to assign a given MAC to a virtual NIC, which is comprised of 2 or more physical NICs in the system. Under these circumstances, it is possible (though not advised) to change the MAC presented by this node to the rest of the network. By default, the software uses the MAC from one of the physical NICs (usually the first one chosen to be trunked/bonded) and presents this to the network on behalf of the virtual NIC that is configured.

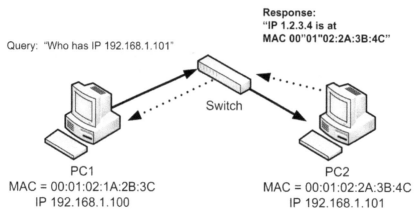

Query: "Who has IP 192.168.1.101"

Response:
"IP 1.2.3.4 is at
MAC 00"01"02:2A:3B:4C"

Switch

PC1
MAC = 00:01:02:1A:2B:3C
IP 192.168.1.100

PC2
MAC = 00:01:02:2A:3B:4C
IP 192.168.1.101

(14) ARP Query and Response

2.4
I've Got Your Number: (Layer 3/Network Layer)

In addition to the MAC, a node must possess at least one Internet Protocol (IP) address in order to communicate with the network. An IP is a string of 12 number separated by dots into four groups of 3 digits each. Unlike the MAC address, which is always unique, the IP address must be unique on the local network (LAN), but need not be unique across the Internet, provided certain other means are in place and working. More on this will follow later.

2.4.1
"Head of the Class": Public vs. Private IP Addresses

We earlier referenced the fact that IP addresses are assigned to one of 3 classes for commercial use: Class A, Class B, and Class C. Each of these classes represents a range of available *public IP addresses*, that is, addresses that are unique across the Internet, and which are (apart from filtering or firewall configurations) accessible from anywhere. Class A IPs are assigned to the largest organizations, Class B to medium-sized organizations, and Class C to small organizations. Within each class, a certain range of addresses is reserved for *private* use, that is, it is not accessible from the public Internet. Private addresses are never routed past a gateway device (router or firewall connecting an organization's internal network to the Internet), and thus can be used within multiple organizations without conflict.

The following table lists the address ranges for the 3 classes, along with the private range within each class. In addition to these, the *loopback* range (127.0.0.0 – 127.255.255.255) is taken from Class A. The *loopback address* commonly used for IPv4 is 127.0.0.0; this IP address should *always* respond to ping.[41]

Class	Full IPv4 Address Range	Private IPv4 Address Range
A	1.0.0.0 – 126.0.0.0	10.0.0.0 – 10.255.255.255
B	128.1.0.0 – 192.254.0.0	172.16.0.0 – 172.31.255.255
C	192.0.1.0 – 223.255.254.0	192.168.0.0 – 192.168.255.255

2.4.2
"Who Is That Masked LAN?":
IP Address Means and Methods

An IP address is comprised of 2 segments, the *network* and the *host*. In addition to the address itself, a *subnet mask* is used to define where the distinction is drawn between the network and the host portions of the address. To understand how the IP address and subnet correlate, consider the following analogy. An accent mark will be used to determine how the word "syllable" is to be pronounced. Shall it be spoken as *sih-LA-buhl*, or *SIHL-uh-buhl*? If written with an accent mark, the first word could be rendered sylláble, with the accent mark putting emphasis on the second part of the word, while the second would be written sỳllable, which emphasizes the first.[42]

With this in mind, consider the anatomy of an IP address and its matching subnet mask. Depending on the class of the address (A, B, or C), the break between the network and host portion of the address will differ, as denoted by the subnet mask

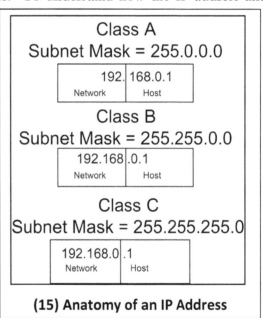

(15) Anatomy of an IP Address

---

[41]Failure to ping the loopback address 127.0.0.0 indicates a problem in the operating system, usually with the TCP/IP stack itself. For instructions on how to reset the TCP/IP stack in Windows, see http://support.microsoft.com/kb/299357.

[42] The analogy is admittedly imperfect, since English does not use accent marks in this way. A better one would use Greek words, but that introduces a whole new complexity. ☺

or CIDR notation. For example, private IP address 192.168.0.1 with subnet mask 255.0.0.0 is a Class A address, with *192.* being the network portion and *168.0.1* the host portion. Conversely, the same IP address with subnet mask 255.255.255.0 becomes a Class C address, with *192.168.0* being the network portion and *.1* the host portion.

Though it is helpful to use an IP address of a given class with the subnet of the same class, this is not required. One common method of addressing private networks is to use the 10.0.0.0 address range (a Class A network) with the Class C subnet mask (255.255.255.0). The resulting subnet offers an IP range of 10.0.0.1 – 10.0.0.254, or 254 hosts. The same IP with a Class A subnet mask, the resulting subnet would contain 16,777,214 hosts! Thus, knowing the subnet mask being used is crucial to configuring a node correctly and/or troubleshooting issues.

2.4.3
The Utopia of a "Classless" Network

German economist and political theorist Karl Marx dreamed of a world in which the social strata of rich and poor, owners and workers, proletariat and *bourgeoisie* would be eliminated, and the world would experience the dawn of a "classless society." Though not as revolutionary, those responsible for overseeing the Internet experienced a similar desire, but for very different reasons. The original method of distributing public IP addresses was inefficient, for it allocated blocks of numbers according to broad ranges (Classes A, B, or C) and then applied a subnet mask to parse the result. By the 1990s, this method of provisioning was found to lack the scalability and flexibility required for the rapidly-growing global Internet. As a result, a new method called *supernetting* was devised, along with a new method of traffic control called *Classless Inter-Domain Routing* (CIDR).

Instead of a subnet mask, CIDR designates *mask bits*. For example, assume that a Class C network in the range of 192.168.1.0 will be configured. The *classful* method would use a subnet mask of 255.255.255.0. This corresponds to 24 *mask bits* in CIDR notation (written as 192.168.1.0/24). Such a network would support a maximum of 256 IP addresses. Note, however, that the first and last numbers of any address range (irrespective of the subnet mask or CIDR) are reserved and cannot be assigned to nodes.[43] For our example, addresses 192.168.1.0 and 192.168.1.255 are therefore unavailable for use, leaving a total of 254 addresses available for nodes on that network.

For private networks, the CIDR method of supernetting is probably overly-complex.

---

[43]For any given subnet, the first IP of the range is the *Subnet ID* (which always has a zero (0) for its last octet) and the last is the *broadcast address*. The *broadcast address* allows packets to be directed to all machines on that subnet, rather than to a specific IP.

Internal networks use address from the private IP ranges (see above). These addresses are never routed to the public Internet, and thus can be used by multiple organizations without conflict.[44] Nonetheless, it is not uncommon to see private addresses written with CIDR notation. When using CIDR notation to a notate a classful subnet, the *mask bits* correspond to the subnet mask for that class, as shown in the table below.

Thus, rather than specifying an IP address of 192.168.1.1 with subnet mask 255.255.255.0, the address can be rendered as 192.168.1.1/24. By knowing the correlation of subnet mask to mask bits, it is easy to recognize a Class A, B, or C network address as such.

Subnet Class	Subnet Mask	CIDR Mask Bits	Usable IP Addresses
A	255.0.0.0	/8	254
B	255.255.0.0	/16	65536
C	255.255.255.0	/24	16777216

Finally, it is important to note that Internet Service Providers (ISPs) sometimes use CIDR notation in documentation. It is therefore important to understand what these designations mean, and have a means for deciphering the settings that might need to be applied to a router or firewall that has a static public IP address.[45]

2.5
Control Freak: TCP vs. UDP

As discussed in Chapter 1, a *frame* is a Layer 2 data unit, while a *packet* is a Layer 3 data unit. When using the Internet Protocol (IP), a packet can use one of two methods for transmitting information. The first and most "popular" is the Transmission Control

---

[44]Note that if two private networks are connected, such as by a dedicated point-to-point connection or VPN, the same rules apply. Subnet 192.168.1.0/24 at location A *cannot* connect to location B if both locations use the same private IP subnet. The workaround to this situation would be either (A) re-configure the subnets, using unique subnets at each location or (B) "hide" the subnets by a means such as Network Address Translation (to be discussed further below). For companies that require information to be shared across the WAN, however, NAT may introduce its own problems, since additional configuration is required to allow the systems at either end to see one another.

[45] A helpful tool can be found at http://www.subnet-calculator.com/cidr.php. The online calculator allows input of an IP address and either the subnet mask (labeled "CIDR Netmask") or Mask Bits. It then outputs various information, including the number of nodes that would be available for that subnet.

Protocol (TCP).[46] The second is the User Datagram Protocol (UDP).

The word *control* in the name of the former is not by accident. TCP—unlike its counterpart, UDP—provides a means of guaranteeing that packets are delivered correctly to the destination. Think of TCP as the tracking system used by your favorite package carrier. For each packet that is sent, a response is returned to the sender to confirm proper delivery. But TCP does more than simply deliver packets to the other end of the wire. Part of the TCP protocol is *flow control*. When communication is initiated between nodes, they first exchange a few salutatory bits of information, and then when this is completed, begin sending packets back and forth, as may be required.

As packets start to move, flow control begins to do its job. If the destination node is unable to keep up with the rate at which packets are being delivered, it may start dropping packets. The sender is then notified that packets are being dropped and/or backlogged at the destination, and is able to resend missing packets or slow the rate at which new ones are transmitted. Flow control is crucial for applications such as web browsing (HTTP or HTTPS), email (SMTP), the File Transfer Protocol (FTP), and other applications that require connection-based, consistent data exchange.

By contrast, UDP does not perform any flow control; as a result, UDP is capable of transmitting data at a faster rate, but with increased risk of dropped packets or collisions. This risk is acceptable due to the nature of the applications that are built upon UDP, for while it is important that a webpage, email, or other file arrive intact and uncorrupted, the same is not true for streaming media (audio/video). The reason for this is simple: the flow control used as part of TCP would cause undue *latency* (lag or delay) in the transmission. UDP is able to stream the massive amounts of data necessary to make voice- or video-over IP a possibility, with an acceptable loss and retransmission rate.

Aside from flow control, TCP also ensures that packets arrive in proper order. Because TCP cannot tolerate missing or out-of-sequence packets, each packet is assigned a sequence number. As these packets are received at the destination, they are reassembled into the proper sequence. Packets that have been lost due to collision or being dropped along the way are retransmitted by the sender. UDP, by contrast, accepts that packets could be lost and resent, duplicated in transmission, or received out of order. Programs that utilize UDP as their transport protocol should take this into account, and include error correction in the application itself, if needed. In the case of voice-over-IP (VoIP), however, a certain degree of packet loss is acceptable, because the error correction and flow control mechanisms of TCP could cause the transmission rate to slow down, and thus affect the quality of the application.

For example, it would be unacceptable for a VoIP telephone system to "wait" while a

---

[46] The popularity of this protocol is reflected in the term TCP/IP, which stands for … you guessed it … the *Transmission Control Protocol/Internet Protocol*.

dropped, malformed, or out-of-sequence packet is resent from IP telephone A to IP telephone B. Nonetheless, in "real-time" applications, a certain degree of delay is assumed and accounted for. Variance from this norm is known as "jitter." To overcome this, *buffers* are used to help regulate and sustain the flow of information. A buffer is a portion of memory set aside to collect packets and queue them up for processing. For example, while the user hears the packets already received and processed (i.e., the words of the caller converted into bits and then back into analog sounds through the earpiece or speaker), the buffer already holds the next set of packets. This helps to maintain a steady and even pace of data flow and ensure that the callers can hear and understand each other. Interruptions to this flow caused by jitter is experienced by the end-users as a stutter or stop/start in the voice or video transmission.

2.6
Have You Been Served? (IP Ports and Services)

Just as computers are physically connected to an Ethernet port (on the wall or directly into a network device, such as a switch or router), network applications communicate via a given *port* or ports. In the physical world, a port is an entry point into the network. In the virtual world of IP, ports allow a given IP address to service a number of applications, each of which have their own port. Think of an *IP port* as a channel on a TV or station on the radio, each of which is assigned a number for easy reference. *Services* are programs or applications that run in the background on a computer (usually a server) and "listen" on the network for inbound connections. Each service runs on a given port or ports, of which there are a total of 65,536 for TCP and/or UDP, ranging in number from 0 through 65,535. Common services run on "well-known" port numbers ranging from 0-1023 (ports 0 and 1023 being reserved), while others run on "registered" port numbers ranging from 1024-49151 (ports 1024 and 49151 being reserved). The remainder (ports 49152-65535) are neither "well-known" nor "registered" for use with a particular service, and are left open for developers to use at their discretion with their own applications.

The following table lists various well-known ports and the services that use them:

Port	TCP	UDP	Application
0	TCP	UDP	Reserved
20	TCP		File Transfer Protocol (FTP) Data transfer
21	TCP		File Transfer Protocol (FTP) Control/command
23	TCP	UDP	Secure Shell (SSH)
25	TCP		Simple Mail Transport Protocol (SMTP)
53	TCP	UDP	Domain Name Service (DNS)
80	TCP		Hypertext Transfer Protocol (HTTP)
110	TCP		Post Office Protocol v3 (POP3)
123		UDP	Network Time Protocol (NTP)
137	TCP	UDP	NetBIOS Name Service
138	TCP	UDP	NetBIOS Datagram Service
139	TCP	UDP	NetBIOS Session Service
143	TCP	UDP	Internet Message Access Protocol (IMAP)
389	TCP	UDP	Lightweight Directory Access Protocol (LDAP)
443	TCP		Hypertext Transfer Protocol Secured (HTTPS)
445	TCP		Active Directory SMB file sharing/Windows shares
530	TCP	UDP	Remote Procedure Call (RPC)
1023	TCP	UDP	Reserved
3389	TCP		Remote Desktop Protocol (RDP)

As noted above, a service can use either TCP or UDP port, or both. Moreover, the full range of TCP and UDP ports is available to each IP address assigned to a node. That being said, different services cannot use the same port on the same IP address. For example, if a server is assigned IP 192.168.1.10, it cannot host two different services or applications that both use TCP port 80 (HTTP). However, it *could* use TCP port 80 for HTTP (web server service) and have another service that utilizes UDP port 80. This is unlikely, though, because a developer that follows best practices would not use a well-known port (even if technically available) for a custom application or service. Finally, that same server might also be able to exchange email with other mail servers (SMTP on TCP port 25), as well as communicate with email client applications (Outlook, etc.) over TCP port 110 (POP3) or TCP/UDP ports 143 (IMAP). All of this could be done with a single IP address on the server because each service runs on a different, established TCP or UDP port/socket.

2.6.1
IPs, Ports, and Sockets

In networking terminology, a *socket* is a combination of an IP address and port number used by an application or service to communicate with other nodes on the network. Operating systems such as Windows and UNIX or Linux track the connections made both inbound and outbound, and can display this information using the **netstat** command.

2.7
An Insider's View to a TCP Session

Services that communicate via TCP (such as web browsers, email, and so forth) do so with a process called a *TCP Session*. In order to demonstrate this, the following scenario is offered: a server running a web server application (IIS or Apache) is "listening" for incoming connections on TCP port 80 (HTTP), the port on which web browsers communicate. From a PC, a user opens a web browser and types in a URL. The browser issues a GET command (the Layer 7 or Application Layer method of requesting a webpage). This command is encapsulated and passed down through the OSI stack to the Data Link Layer, where it formed into a frame that is to be transmitted to the server.

In order to send this frame, PC must initiate a TCP connection with Server. This connection is established via a 3-way exchange of information called a *handshake*. PC first sends a *synchronization* packet to Server, indicating that it wishes to open a channel for data exchange. This packet is transmitted to the IP of Server, and must be sent over the appropriate port number, in this case, TCP port 80. If Server is able to open such a channel, it responds with a *synchronization acknowledgement* (SYN-ACK). The sending node (PC) then sends its own acknowledgement (ACK) to confirm that it received and understood the reply.

Thereafter, the communication channel is opened and transmission of data packets ensues. During this stage of the TCP Session, Server may instruct PC to either send more or less packets at a time. This is part of the flow control functionality of TCP, and ensures that packets are not lost in transit. As packets are sent by PC and received by Server, the acknowledgement (ACK) from Server includes a bit of information called a *TCP Window*. The window is the size (in bytes) that the destination node is able to accept at one time; this is the Session layer (Layer 4) equivalent to the *Maximum Transmission Unit* (MTU) at the Network layer (Layer 2). The higher this TCP Windows number, the more information is sent at one time, and the more efficient and effective the network utilization for this TCP session. If collisions, dropped packets, or out-of-sequence packets are encountered, the destination (Server) may reply with an ACK that lowers the TCP Window, thus limiting the connection speed while it plays catch-up.

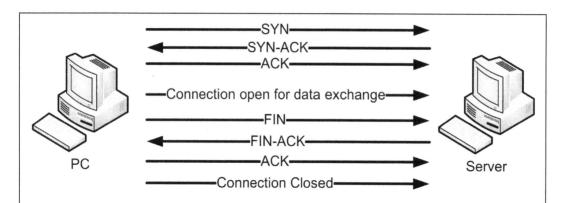

The server is "listening" for incoming connections on TCP port 80 (HTTP).

From the PC, a user opens a web browser and types in a URL.

The browser issues a GET (Application Layer) which is translated down the OSI stack into a transmittable frame of data.

In order to send this frame, the PC must initiate a TCP connection with the server. This connection is established via a 3-way exchange of information called a *handshake*.

SYN = Synchronization ("I have data for you.")
SYN-ACK = Acknowledgement of received SYN ("Very well.")
ACK = Acknowledgement of the SYN-ACK ("OK, here goes.")
[Data exchange proceeds]
FIN = Finish ("OK, I'm done")
FIN-ACK = Acknowledgement from destination of FIN ("OK, goodbye!")
ACK = Acknowledgement from sender of FIN-ACK ("Goodbye!")
[Connection is closed]

(16) A TCP Session

CHAPTER 3:
NETWORK DESIGN AND PRACTICE

3.1
Up and Down and Side-To-Side

A network is said to be either *flat* or *hierarchical*. A flat network is comprised of a single group of computers using the same subnet or range of IP addresses. For example, consider a network that uses the IP address schema 192.168.1.0/24 (a Class C network of not more than 256 nodes). Devices on this network would use ARP (Address Resolution Protocol; see Chapter 2 above) to determine each other's IPs. A hierarchical network, like the domain name space, is more like a pyramid, in which a top level network gives way to one or more additional networks (subnets and/or segments). Traffic in a flat network topology is essentially "side-to-side," that is, between nodes connected to the same switch

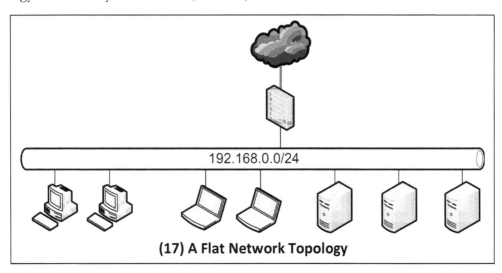

(17) A Flat Network Topology

or switches. Conversely, traffic in a hierarchical topology can be side-to-side within a given segment, or "up-and-down" between segments.

Note that in this *flat* topology, all nodes (servers, PCs, laptops) are connected to a single Ethernet subnet/segment, using a single Class C IP address range of 192.168.0.0. Following common practice, the inside interface of the firewall would probably be addressed as 192.168.0.1. Other nodes could be addressed however desired. All nodes are connected to the Internet via the firewall, which is locally attached. Thus, internal nodes would have access to resources on the public Internet (provided such access is allowed by the firewall rules).

In an *hierarchical* topology, nodes are connected to different subnets/segments, perhaps organized by floor, department, or job function. The 192.168.0.0/24 is the "root" network into which all others connect, and through which all others would communicate. The root network is also connected to the Internet, and thus acts as the gateway for all internal nodes to access resources there (again, subject to applicable firewall rules).

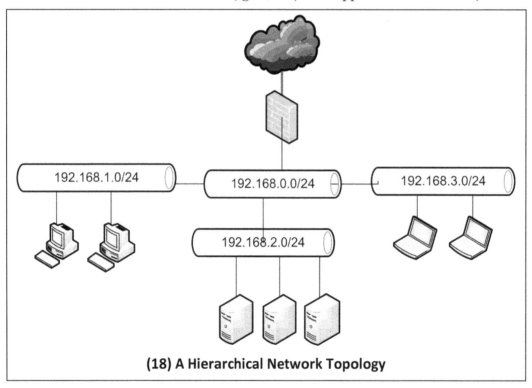

(18) A Hierarchical Network Topology

3.2
Segments and Subnets

As a network grows, it may be necessary to create *subnets* or *segments*. A *segment* is a physical subdivision of a network created for security, performance, or administrative reasons. A *subnet* is a logical subdivision of a network created for the same reason. Thus, a segment exists in hardware, while a subnet exists in software.

Consider the network diagram below. Subnet 1 contains user computers and a network printer. Subnet 2 contains servers. The subnets are connected via a router. Both subnets are then connected from the router to the firewall, and out to the Internet. One can surmise that the network was divided into segments for security purposes, because the servers are on Subnet 2, while the user machines are on Subnet 1. The router is the *gateway device* between them, allowing a computer on Subnet 1 to connect to the file server or email server on Subnet 2.

For a small network, such a configuration may be overly-complex. For a larger network, however, it provides a means for segmenting traffic as well as providing security. This diagram thus depicts a small network that has been segmented internally for whatever

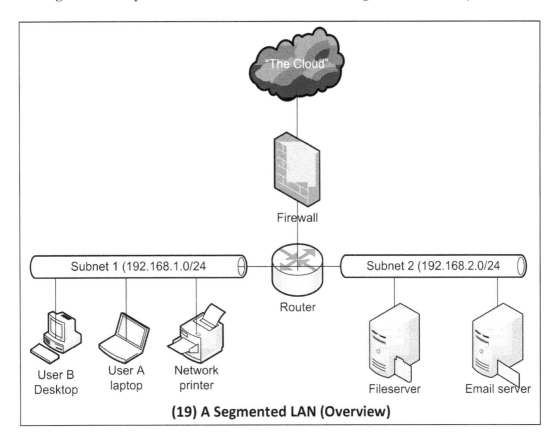

(19) A Segmented LAN (Overview)

reason: security, performance, or perhaps both.

The simplest network always contains at least one segment and one subnet. Large networks may contain many segments and multiple subnets. For example, consider an office building with many floors. Each floor could be a network segment and subnet. These would, in turn, be connected to a central router or routing switch that provides physical connectivity (ports) for the various segments and enables communication between the subnets through routing. (These terms will be explored more in future sections.)

3.3
Switches and Routers and Gateways (Oh My!)

Whether flat or hierarchical, the heart of a LAN is a device called a switch. As detailed above, an Ethernet packet contains both a destination and source address. A *switch* (also called a *switching hub*) is capable of reading the header information of the Ethernet packets that traverse its interfaces. This is a fancy way of saying that as a packet enters the switch on Port 1, it can read the information of the packet and determine that it its destination is a device whose MAC Address is known to be connected to Port 2 on that same switch. If the destination address of the packet corresponds to a known entity (locally attached), the switch is thus able to direct traffic to the appropriate port (physical interface) that connects to the destination device with that MAC address. This is possible, again, because the switch maintains a *table* of the MAC addresses it has discovered on the various interfaces to which it has connectivity.

In the diagram above, the switch has read the MAC address of frames coming from its connected interfaces and added this information, along with the hostname and IP address of the device sending the frames, to its MAC Address Table. Using this information, it is then able to route traffic between connected devices.

Switches are classified as either *unmanaged* or *managed* (a.k.a., "intelligent"). Both can read the MAC Address of frames it receives, and forward them on to the appropriate port. Beyond that, however, the *unmanaged switch* is a silent party, in that it cannot be assigned an IP address of its own nor be monitored or controlled. A *managed switch*, conversely, can be assigned an IP address and is capable of providing information about Layers 1-3 of the frames that traverse its interfaces. For example, a managed switch offers a Graphical User Interface (GUI) or Command Line Interface (CLI) by which the switch can be configured and monitored. Though these interfaces, an administrator can view or configure information about the physical interfaces on the switch, as well as view logs or other troubleshooting information that may be collected. A managed switch thus has a more sophisticated processor and operating system than an unmanaged switch.

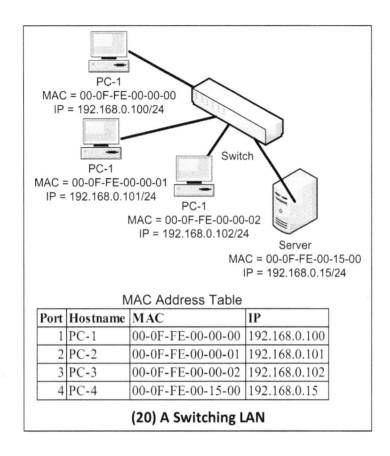

Port	Hostname	MAC	IP
1	PC-1	00-0F-FE-00-00-00	192.168.0.100
2	PC-2	00-0F-FE-00-00-01	192.168.0.101
3	PC-3	00-0F-FE-00-00-02	192.168.0.102
4	PC-4	00-0F-FE-00-15-00	192.168.0.15

(20) A Switching LAN

3.3.1
Switching and Routing

Switches are able to read the MAC and route the frame to another connected device, but what if the IP for which this packet is intended is not on the same switch or even the local network? Here we step into the world of *routing*. Before proceeding, however, the introduction of some terms is in order. (More will be said about these in the sections to follow.)

Referenced above, a *subnet* is a logical group of network devices. It is logical because these devices use the same IP address range (as determined by the *subnet mask* or CIDR mask bits). A *segment* is a physical division within the network, usually for security purposes. A *route* is a path from one subnet or network segment to another. A *default gateway* is the virtual door that tells the operating system of a given node how to access nodes that are not on its local subnet. For example, Node A with IP of 192.168.1.100 needs to access files on Node B at IP 192.168.2.50. Since the nodes are on different subnets, they cannot "see" each other at Layer 2 of the network.[47] The means by which Node A and Node B are able to communicate is through a device called a *router*. A router operates at Layer 3 of the OSI model (Data Link Layer) and is able to see not only the MAC Address information of a packet, but the IP information as well.[48] Like a switch, a router always has multiple (at least 2) interfaces or NICs. Unlike a switch, however, a router is a *gateway device* or *perimeter device*. A switch is literally at the center of things (recall the star topology from Chapter 1 above), for it is the point into which nodes connect. The router, conversely, is the "gateway" to another network, and so exists at the "perimeter" of a given network. To review:

- *Segments* are physical divisions within a network, usually created for geographic or security reasons.
- *Subnets* are logical divisions based on ranges of IP addresses being used.
- A network that is segmented and/or subnetted must allow for connectivity between those segments/subnets. This connectivity involves establishing *routes*.
- A *router* is a Layer 3 device that connects 2 or more subnets (which operate at Layer 2) together. As such, it is the *gateway* or *perimeter* of those networks.

3.3.2
The Mechanics of IP Routing

We have said that Layer 2 devices connect through a router, which operates at Layer 3. But how will a node on Subnet A know how to connect to the router that is also connected to Subnet B? The answer is through use of a software configuration called the *default gateway*.

---

[47] It is possible to have multiple subnets share the same physical segment, such as a switch. This is not a best practice for several reasons. First, segmentation is often done for security reasons. Since the machines share the same physical segment and broadcast domain, it would be possible to "spoof" MAC or IP addresses and cross-connect a PC into the alternate subnet. Because there is no impediment to this, such a topology would undermine any security that was intended.

Secondly, and more importantly, unless such "spoofing" were employed, the 2 subnets would still be unable to "see" each other. ARP is restricted to a given subnet, so even if nodes A and B (using different subnet IPs) were in the same broadcast domain, they would never cross-populate each other's MAC address tables. As a result, the machines would not be able to communicate, even though they were connected to the same switch.

[48] Recall that the Internet Protocol (IP) and its related protocols exist at Layer 3.

When the NIC is configured on a node, the following information must be included:

- IP Address
- Subnet Mask
- [Default Gateway]

Note that the default gateway is in brackets. Technically, it is not required to enter this information in order to connect a node to the network. If the network is isolated—that is, it is not connected to other networks—then the default gateway is not required, and may not even exist. In order for this subnet or LAN to be connected to other subnets or LANs, however, the default gateway must exist and must be configured in the NIC settings of all the nodes.

What, then, is the *default gateway*? In short, it is the IP address of the device (router) that connects to other (or another) subnet(s) or network(s). That device might, in turn, have its own default gateway that is used to connect to still other networks or subnets. Obviously, for connectivity to work properly, all of this must be functioning as designed. From the perspective of a given node, however, the only thing that matters is that *its* default gateway be assigned properly. What happens farther up the chain is beyond its control.

Switches and other network devices often have a different term for the same concept: the *default route*. Like the default gateway, the default route is the interface of a router that is capable of reaching other networks. Unlike a default gateway, however, the router does not have this as its only choice. From the perspective of the node, the default gateway is the means by which it communicates with other nodes that are not on its subnet. A router, however, may be connected to multiple subnets. The default route is therefore the last-resort path for traffic that does not exist on any of its network interfaces (NICs). This information is stored in a *routing table* (the Layer 3 complement to the MAC Address table for Layer 2) and used to make decisions as to which interface a given packet should be routed, one of which is on the same subnet as the default route IP address.

A true routing device operates as Layer 3, but a switch may have limited capabilities called *static routing*. The difference is that *static routing* requires manual programming of the information for a routing table, while a true Layer 3 device discerns this automatically. Static routes are also limited in their capabilities, both from performance and connectivity. For a simple network topology, however, it may be perfectly adequate.

A *Layer 3 switch* or *routing switch* is what the name describes: a switch into which full routing functionality has been added. As a switch, it will read and forward packets based on the source and destination addresses in the TCP header. As a router, however, it is capable of not only interconnecting 2 or more subnets (like the static routes configuration of the Layer 2 switch described above), but of maintaining a truly *dynamic* routing table.

Layer 3 switches have become popular in LANs where multiple segments and subnets have been designed, as a replacement for traditional routers. The tradeoff is that a routing switch is not designed (nor capable) of the high performance of a dedicated router.[49]

The diagram below depicts a network that has been divided into 3 segments/subnets:

Subnet 1 for user devices
Subnet 2 for internal servers
Subnet 3 leading to the public Internet

In our example, Subnet3 is a *Demilitarized Zone* (DMZ)—that is, a lower-security subnet into which access is granted from the Internet. Just as a switch builds and maintains the *MAC Address Table* from the information it gleans from the devices connected to it, so a router builds a *Routing Table*. In the case of a router, each of these interfaces (NICs) is configured with a separate IP address and subnet mask, corresponding to the subnet to which it is connected. It then determines the best *route* for packets passing from one subnet to another. For example, if a

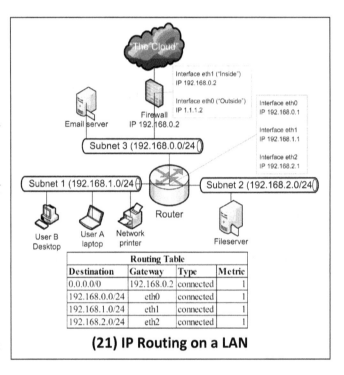

(21) IP Routing on a LAN

device on Subnet 1 wishes to communicate with the fileserver on Subnet 2, the traffic it sends must be routed accordingly. The router receives the frames on its interface named eth1, which has the IP of 192.168.1.1. It then opens and unpacks the frame in order to reads the Layer 3 information contained (*encapsulated*) therein. With this accomplished, it knows the destination IP address to which the packet is addressed. The IP data payload is then encapsulated in a frame by the router and forwarded to the IP specified, sending the data out the interface named "eth2" with IP address 192.168.2.1, the interface that is connected to Subnet 2.

---

[49] Internet Service Providers handling traffic for the public Internet would use dedicated (and large!) routers, which are capable of processing high-volume traffic. Layer 3 switches, conversely, might be found as the "core" of a multi-subnet LAN.

3.3.3
Routes and Gateways

The diagram expands upon our previous example. Note that the default route for Subnet 1 or Subnet 2 is interface 1 or interface 2, respectively. In other words, the default gateway is the interface on the router (perimeter or gateway device) that corresponds to its subnet. For the sake of simplicity, the network designer has assigned the ".1" node address to the router for each subnet. The firewall, in turn, is configured with 2 interfaces. The "Inside" interface (eth1) has been assigned private IP 192.168.0.2. Note that this is also the default route for the router. The "Outside" interface (eth0) is configured with IP 2.2.2.2. Finally, a default route has been configured on the firewall, pointing to IP address 2.2.2.1. This configuration allows traffic to be routed end-to-end from a node on one of the private subnets to a destination on the public Internet, and back.

3.4
Network Address Translation

3.4.1
Static NAT

As previously mentioned, a private IP address is never routed on the public Internet. This is so because they are not intended to be unique. Thus, XYZ Corporation may use the internal IP scheme of 192.168.0.1/24. However, across the street, ABC Company may use the same network topology for their internal systems. Even though both companies are connected to the Internet, the two subnets will not conflict with each other because they are using private addresses that are never routed outside their own LAN.[50]

Very well, then how does a user whose workstation does not have a public IP address browse the "Net?" The answer is simply: by the magic of *Network Address Translation*, or NAT.[51] A NAT rule is configured on a firewall (or router with firewall functionality) as either *static* or *dynamic*. A *static* NAT configuration maps a single public IP to a single private IP, and is commonly used in conjunction with Access Control Lists (ACLs) to grant access to resources on the private network from the public Internet. For example, a

---

[50] The caveat to this is that the two networks are not connected by a private "backdoor" link, such as a leased line or VPN tunnel. Were this to exist, having the same subnets defined on both sides of the street would indeed conflict; indeed, it would lead to strange behavior and error messages popping up everywhere!

[51] Given what has come before, the reader may view "NAT" as an acronym for "Not Another Term!"

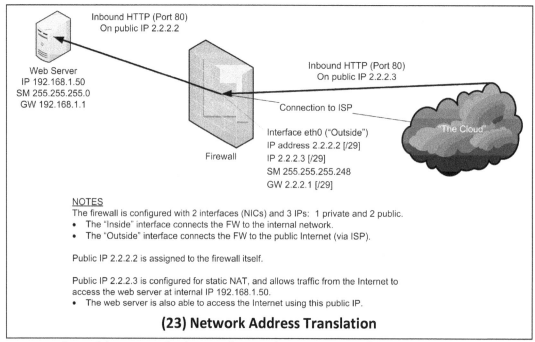

Inbound HTTP (Port 80)
On public IP 2.2.2.2

Web Server
IP 192.168.1.50
SM 255.255.255.0
GW 192.168.1.1

Inbound HTTP (Port 80)
On public IP 2.2.2.3

Connection to ISP

"The Cloud"

Interface eth0 ("Outside")
IP address 2.2.2.2 [/29]
IP 2.2.2.3 [/29]
SM 255.255.255.248
GW 2.2.2.1 [/29]

Firewall

NOTES
The firewall is configured with 2 interfaces (NICs) and 3 IPs: 1 private and 2 public.
- The "Inside" interface connects the FW to the internal network.
- The "Outside" interface connects the FW to the public Internet (via ISP).

Public IP 2.2.2.2 is assigned to the firewall itself.

Public IP 2.2.2.3 is configured for static NAT, and allows traffic from the Internet to access the web server at internal IP 192.168.1.50.
- The web server is also able to access the Internet using this public IP.

(23) Network Address Translation

company that wishes to make its email or web server accessible from outside the firewall would configure the perimeter device (firewall or router) for NAT, assigning a dedicated public IPs to be mapped to the static private IP of the server. The ACL would then determine what ports are "open," i.e., on which ports traffic is allowed to pass through the firewall from the outside to the inside.

The firewall is configured with 2 interfaces (NICs) and 3 IP addresses. The "Inside" interface connects the FW to the internal network. The "Outside" interface connects the FW to the public Internet (via ISP). Public IP 2.2.2.2 is assigned to the firewall itself on the "Outside" interface. Public IP 2.2.2.3 is configured for static NAT, and allows traffic from the Internet to access the web server at internal IP 192.168.1.50. The web server is also able to access the Internet using this public IP.

Suppose that a packet sent from port 80 reaches the firewall on IP address 2.2.2.3. The packet is identified as an HTTP request (GET), which is seeking to download a page from a website hosted on the Web Server. Assuming a firewall rule is in place to allow this, the packet would enter the firewall on the Outside interface and connect to the backend server. In the configuration depicted above, the port number is the same for both the internal and external IPs: TCP port 80, or HTTP. (Recall that for any given application or service, both the IP address (source or destination) and port number must be known. As the reply from the server is then sent out, it too is *translated* to look like it came from the *external* IP.

3.4.2
Network Address Port Translation (Dynamic NAT)

As the scenario above shows, a static NAT configuration establishes a 1:1 relationship between an internal IP/port and an external IP/port. Thus, any traffic sent to outside IP 2.2.2.3 on port 80 is routed through the firewall to inside IP 192.168.2.50 on port 80. Conversely, a *dynamic* NAT configuration maps a range of private IPs to a single public IP, using different port numbers for each outbound connection in order to allow for simultaneous "conversations" between internal and external computers. In the process, the internal IP of the source machine is "hidden" by the public IP configured for dynamic NAT. Dynamic Nat is also called *Network Address Port Translation* (NAPT).[52] Regardless of the term used, the methodology is the same. An inside IP address wishes to send packets through the firewall to the network(s) on the other side (probably the public Internet). When the packet reaches the firewall, it is examined for the following information:

- Source IP
- Destination IP
- Source port (TCP/UDP)
- Destination port (TCP/UDP)

The diagram below visualizes how these processes work. In this example, the firewall is configured with 2 interfaces (NICs) and 2 IPs: 1 private and 2 public. The "Inside" interface connects the FW to the internal network. The "Outside" interface connects the FW to the public Internet (via ISP). Public IP 2.2.2.2 is assigned to the firewall itself, but is also configured for dynamic NAT, which allows the PC at internal IP 192.168.1.100 to connect to the Internet. Packets sent from the PC are modified ("translated") at the firewall to use a header containing the outside IP 2.2.2.2, then transmitted to the Internet.

In this scenario, the PC initiates an outbound connection using TCP 80 (HTTP) to a website hosted at IP 1.2.3.4. When the packets reach the firewall, *Network Address Port Translation* (NATP, also called *Dynamic NAT*) is applied. First, the source IP is changed from the internal IP (192.168.1.100) to the external IP of the firewall (2.2.2.3), which is also being used for NAT. Second, the source port is changed from 80 to 3000. (Port 3000 falls within the range of unassigned ports, and is used here for a dynamic connection.) This makes the packet look like it came from a host with IP 2.2.2.3, sending packets on TCP port 3000; the actual IP of the internal node (PC) has been "translated."

---

[52]The terms *dynamic* and *static* for NAT are adopted from usage on Check Point firewalls. In the world of Cisco firewalls, static NAT is referred to simply as NAT, while dynamic NAT is called *Port Address Translation* (PAT).

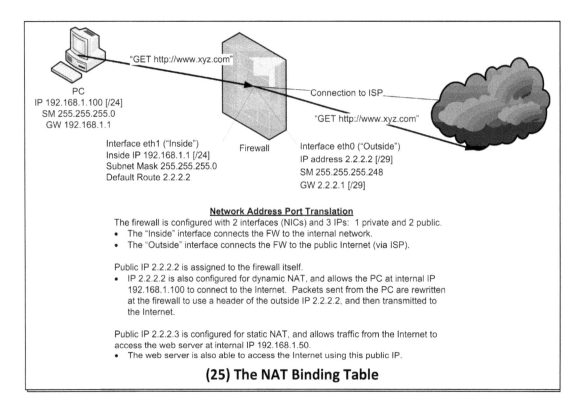

Network Address Port Translation

The firewall is configured with 2 interfaces (NICs) and 3 IPs: 1 private and 2 public.
- The "Inside" interface connects the FW to the internal network.
- The "Outside" interface connects the FW to the public Internet (via ISP).

Public IP 2.2.2.2 is assigned to the firewall itself.
- IP 2.2.2.2 is also configured for dynamic NAT, and allows the PC at internal IP 192.168.1.100 to connect to the Internet. Packets sent from the PC are rewritten at the firewall to use a header of the outside IP 2.2.2.2, and then transmitted to the Internet.

Public IP 2.2.2.3 is configured for static NAT, and allows traffic from the Internet to access the web server at internal IP 192.168.1.50.
- The web server is also able to access the Internet using this public IP.

(25) The NAT Binding Table

At the same time, the NAT service on the firewall writes an entry into its *NAT Binding Table*. In short, the binding table is a cross-reference of associations made by the NAT service between an inside IP/port and an external IP/port. The NAT service writes the internal IP (192.168.1.100) to the table, but assigns it a port value of 2000. The outside IP is 2.2.2.3 is assigned port 3000. The packet is then transmitted to the remote server. When the Server receives the packets, it interprets the request and answers on TCP port 80. (The other machine answers on the port to which the packet was sent.) In so doing, however, it responds to the "translated" IP it sees in the source header of the packets it has just processed. Thus, the response is sent to IP 2.2.2.3 on TCP port 3000.

When these packets reach the firewall, the NAT software does a lookup on the binding table to determine what internal IP/port corresponds to the destination information it sees in the packet header. From the binding table, it sees that external IP 2.2.2.3 with port 3000 corresponds to internal IP 192.168.1.100 with port 2000. It therefore "translates" the packet by once again rewriting the header information and changing the destination IP/port combination. The packet is then received by the PC and processed accordingly.

The true power of NAPT comes when multiple internal services or devices are communicating with multiple outside resources. A single machine, for example, might have several applications exchanging information with various servers on the Internet. Each of these communications would be "translated" through the dynamic NAT. In addition, if multiple PCs were all connecting to a website, each communication channel would be controlled by dynamic NAT, with auto-assigned port numbers to track which responses from the remote machine needs to be forwarded to which internal node.

3.5
"None Shall Pass":
An Introduction to Firewalls

3.5.1
Router vs. Firewall

In building construction, a "firewall" is a wall that uses special fireproof materials to contain or segment a building. The purpose of the firewall is, as its names suggests, to block advance of a fire. In the context of networking, a firewall does something similar: it segments or blocks off a subnet, network, or series of networks from other networks. Note that this is precisely the opposite use as a router, which enables traffic to pass between 2 or more subnets or networks unhindered, and in fact provides the bridge between them. A network firewall necessarily includes routing functionality, but in addition, is designed to provide traffic control.

3.5.2
Perimeter Firewall

A firewall is most commonly placed at the *perimeter* of the LAN, that is, between the internal machines and the Internet. As a gateway device with at least basic routing capabilities, the firewall is configured for one or more external (public) IPs and/or internal (private) IPs. Finally, an *Access Control List* (ACL) determines what traffic is allowed to pass through the firewall. The ACL must include the following information:

- Source IP ("from" address)
- Destination IP ("to" address)
- Port type (TCP or UDP)
- Port number

Depending on the operating system used, ACLs may be configured using the command-line interface (CLI) or graphical user interface (GUI). If CLI is used, ACLs may be displayed as simple text; if GUI, rules may be represented by objects, with visual

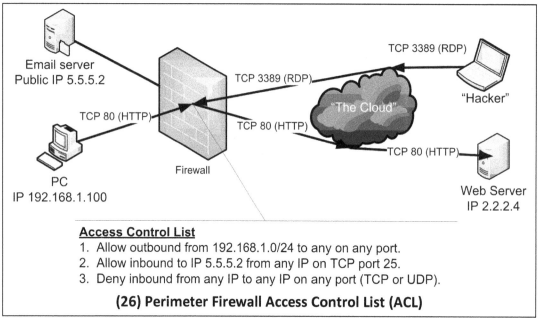

Access Control List
1. Allow outbound from 192.168.1.0/24 to any on any port.
2. Allow inbound to IP 5.5.5.2 from any IP on TCP port 25.
3. Deny inbound from any IP to any IP on any port (TCP or UDP).

(26) Perimeter Firewall Access Control List (ACL)

representation of their relationships. Regardless of the methodology employed, the result is a rule base by which the firewall software determines what packets are permitted, and which are denied, on a given interface. On a simple firewall with 2 interfaces (*Inside* for the private LAN and *Outside* for the Internet-facing network), the default configuration on most firewalls is to allow all outbound traffic and deny all inbound traffic. That is, a device on the private network is allowed to connect to the Internet on any TCP or UDP port (such as TCP 80, or HTTP web browsing).

In the example below, the PC initiates an outbound request from the web browser, pointing to a URL that resolves to IP 2.2.2.4. This reaches the firewall and is subject to the rules configured. In this case, outbound traffic (that is, traffic originating from the subnet for which the Inside interface is configured) is allowed for TCP port 80. The packet is therefore "translated" via NAT and allowed to enter The Cloud, where it finds the web server at IP 2.2.2.4. At the same time, a would-be hacker attempts to connect via the Remote Desktop Protocol (RDP), which uses TCP port 3389, to the email server whose public IP is 5.5.5.2. However, the firewall only allows inbound connections to this IP address on TCP port 25 (SMTP). Thus, the attempted connection is blocked at the firewall and is neither translated by NAT nor allowed to pass beyond the outside interface. (At Hacker's laptop, the RDP client hangs with an hour-glass and finally returns an error that the connection could not be established.)

When a reply to the web browsing session for PC are received on the Outside interface, the firewall checks its connection tables and determines that this is a reply to data initiated from inside, and authorized during a previous connection. It is therefore processed for NAT and sent through to the internal machine.

FOUNDATIONS OF WINDOWS NETWORKING

3.5.3
The State of the Firewall

First-generation firewalls were *stateless*, that is, they did not control or even track the connections made through them. Rather, these firewalls were based on the concept of *packet filtering*, whereby network packets traversing the firewall were subject to certain rules that governed whether a given packet destined for a given IP/port combination was legitimate. Packet filtering was fast, for it occurred at the Network Layer (Layer 3), and read only enough information from the packet headers to drop the packet or forward it on. However, a stateless firewall was incapable of determining whether a given packet was part of a previous conversation, starting a new one, or simply an attacker trying to slip through the perimeter. As such, stateless firewalls were targets for spoofing, whereby packets were transmitted from somewhere other than the legitimate sender, but made to look like they were valid.

By contrast, modern firewalls are *stateful*, and capable of tracking the *state* of the connections passing through it. By participating in the "handshake" that establishes the connection (see Chapter 2 above), the firewall is able to determine whether a given packet is part of an existing connection, starting a new one, or simply a rogue agent to be unceremoniously dispatched. In order to do this, the firewall requires a considerable amount of CPU and memory resources, for it keeps information about the various connections memory-resident.

3.5.4
The Ubiquitous Broadband Router/Firewall/Switch

An aside is necessary at this point. In the era of inexpensive and widely-available broadband, it is common to refer to device used simply as a "firewall" or "router." To be more precise, however, the device in question is, in fact, a combination of three devices: an Ethernet switch, a router, and a firewall. The diagram illustrates this principle.

The device at the center of the diagram is a representation of a typical Small Office Home Office (SOHO) device that provides basic firewall and routing functionality to a broadband (cable or DSL) internet provider. The device also includes a 4-port switch into which internal network devices would be connected. The diagram also depicts a 2nd Ethernet switch connected to the SOHO router/firewall to allow for more than the 4 network ports.

In addition to, and separate from, the 4-port switch, is the WAN or Internet uplink port. The firewall depicted above is actually a Cisco PIX 501. As with all Cisco devices (and those by other manufacturers), network interfaces are numbered sequentially starting with zero.

Interface0 (sometimes labeled *eth0* or simply *e0*) is usually connected to the WAN, while other ports (starting with interface1) are connected to internal network devices or switches. Note that interface0 is connected to a DSL or cable modem, which converts the signal from the Internet Service Provider (ISP) into Ethernet. The modem would thus have an RJ45 jack for connection to the firewall/router, and another

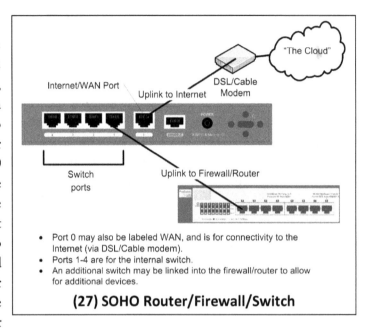

- Port 0 may also be labeled WAN, and is for connectivity to the Internet (via DSL/Cable modem).
- Ports 1-4 are for the internal switch.
- An additional switch may be linked into the firewall/router to allow for additional devices.

(27) SOHO Router/Firewall/Switch

connection (coax for cable or RJ11 for DSL) for connection to the provider's network.

3.6
DHCP: The Dynamic Host Configuration Protocol

In the world of TCP/IP and Ethernet, each node must have a unique address IP address in order to properly communicate with the network. In the early days, assignment of these IPs was done manually. The advantage here is that each machine becomes a known entity (provided, of course, that proper documentation is maintained to avoid IP conflicts). It also means, however, that any changes necessary to the configuration of those nodes must also be done manually. For small networks that are relative static (i.e., that do not change often), this can work fine. The same method applied to larger, more dynamic networks, however, may prove to be untenable. It is for this reason that a new service was developed that allowed nodes to automatically be assigned an address, derived from a list of available addresses, and preconfigured with certain other settings that allow it to properly connect to and navigate the network. This service is the *Dynamic Host Configuration Protocol* (DHCP).

DHCP works by dynamically assigning IP addresses to client machines on the network. These IP assignments are limited in duration, however, insofar as they "expire." The duration of time for which the IP is valid is called a *lease*.

3.6.1
DHCP Discovery

A client computer is configured for DHCP in the network settings of the operating system. On startup, reboot, or whenever the network connectivity is established (i.e., the NIC senses connectivity to the network), it begins to broadcast using UDP port 67 in search of a DHCP server. This phase is called *DHCP Discovery*.

When a DHCP server receives this broadcast, it responds with a *DHCP offer*, which includes the following information:

- MAC address of the client machine
- IP address and subnet mask to be assigned
- Lease duration
- IP address of the DHCP server making the offer

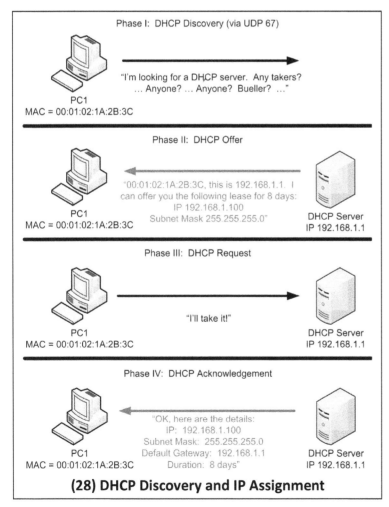

(28) DHCP Discovery and IP Assignment

If multiple servers are present on the network, each may make an offer. The client will accept only one of these offers and then broadcast a DHCP *request*. This broadcast messages accomplishes two things. First, it acknowledges that it will accept the IP address being offered from a given DHCP server. Secondly, it notifies all other DHCP servers that it is being assigned an IP from the server whose offer it accepted. (In general, the offer is accepted from the first DHCP server that responds.) The final stage is the *DHCP acknowledgement*, in which the DHCP server that extended the accepted offer transmits the lease duration and other information requested by the client.

At this point, the IP is assigned to that node. Once the operating system completes its own tasks of binding the IP to the NIC, the node begins communicating on the network. Meanwhile, the DHCP server writes the assignment information to its database, to ensure that the same IP is not assigned to another client.

The power of DHCP lies in the flexibility it brings. Aside from the basics, such as IP address and subnet mask, a DHCP client can be automatically configured with a default gateway, DNS server IPs, and other information that is necessary for it to successfully navigate a network. For example, suppose DHCP is used for all PCs. DNS servers with IP address 1.1.1.1 and 1.1.1.2 are to be used with all nodes on the network. DHCP servers are therefore configured to include this information for distribution to all DHCP clients. If in the future this configuration changes—say, a third DNS server at IP 1.1.1.3 is added—this information can be included in the DHCP configuration. Whenever a lease expires for a client, it will begin the DHCP Discovery phase anew, at the end of which—assuming all goes as designed—it will receive an IP address. Along with this IP (either the same or different than before), it will also receive the updated DNS configuration.

3.6.2
DHCP Release and Renew

Under normal circumstances, a DHCP client will initiate a discovery whenever it powers on or reboots, loses and regains connectivity to the network (i.e., an Ethernet cable is removed and then reconnected), or certain changes are made to the network settings. Thereafter, it should continue to operate with the IP as assigned by the DHCP server until the lease expires. If this configuration requires a refresh before that time—such as the scenario above, where a new DNS server is added and should be updated on all clients—a DHCP client can be forced to initiate a discovery manually. This process is called *release* and *renew*.

The release does what it says: notifies the DHCP server that it no longer wishes to use the IP assigned. The client thereafter deactivates its IP address and the DHCP server removes the configuration entry from its database. It is important to note that simply unplugging the Ethernet cable from a node should *not* initiate a DHCP release. Rather, the node will initiate a discovery, requesting the previously-used IP, if known, and accepting an offer as provided by a DHCP server. The release function, conversely, *clears* the IP configuration from both the client and the DHCP server. A *DHCP renew* operation then (manually) initiates a discovery phase.

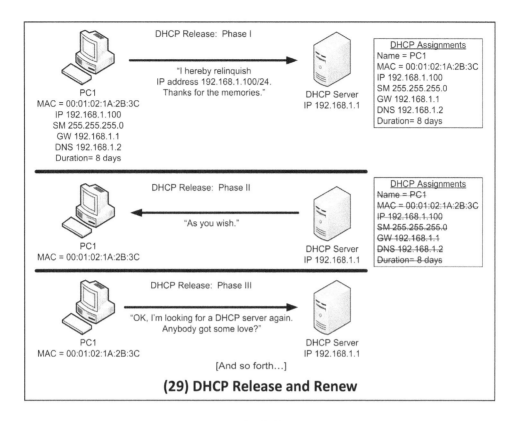

(29) DHCP Release and Renew

3.6.3
DHCP Relay

When DHCP clients and DHCP servers reside on the same subnet, they communicate using UDP broadcast. If the server and clients are on different subnets, however, communication via unicast, that is, directly from machine A to machine B. For this to function properly between subnets, switches and routers must be configured to forward these packets accordingly. This function is called *DHCP relay*, or sometimes *DHCP helper*, and is configured according to the guidelines of the vendor.

3.7
APIPA: The Automatic Private IP Address Service

If you work with Windows machines long enough, you will likely encounter a machine that has an IP address of 169.254.x.x. The observant reader will note that this is not among the listing of IPs reserved by the Internet Assigned Numbers Authority (IANA). Indeed, the IP address range 169.254.0.0 – 169.254.255.255 is a separate group of IP addresses reserved by the IANA for a feature called **Automatic Private IP Addressing (APIPA)**.

Within the Windows platform, APIPA provides a mechanism whereby the machine is automatically assigned an IP from this range if *both* of the following statements are true:

- A static IP is not assigned to the NIC.
- DHCP discovery failed to locate an available DHCP server.

From an administrative or troubleshooting perspective, this makes things interesting, to say the least. Because APIPA is built into Windows, it would be possible to have a group of computers (such as on a peer-to-peer network) with no router or other device to provide DHCP communicate between themselves using APIPA-assigned IP addresses. For this to work, the machines must be on the same LAN (physical network segment, such as a switch or hub) and subnet (logical network segment, i.e., range of IPs). You will notice, further, that the machines would be able to communicate locally *only*; like other private IPs, APIPA is not routable. Unlike the IANA private subnets classes, however, being non-routable means they cannot connect to the Internet, either. Were 2 computers to time-out when trying to contact a DHCP server and both be assigned APIPA IP addresses, they should be able to communicate with each other, but would effectively be isolated from the rest of the world, even if access were possible under other circumstances.

3.7.1
Troubleshooting APIPA[53]

In a situation such as describe above, where computers communicate internally among themselves, but cannot access other resources, the first thing to check would be the IP assignment of the various machines. This is easily accomplished with the **ipconfig** command. If the machines are configured for DHCP, but no server is found, the broadcast/discovery process described above will eventually time-out, and the APIPA address will be used instead. The following is a quick checklist of a possible approach to the situation:

- Verify that a DHCP server is running, and/or restart the service.
- If other machines are working with DHCP, try to isolate the issue to a given machine or network segment. (Perhaps a switch port, NIC or cable is bad?)

---

[53]For more information on APIPA, see:
http://support.microsoft.com/kb/220874.

- Verify that the DHCP server has not used up its address pool. If the server is running, but no IPs are left in the pool, it has nothing left to assign to clients.
- If the DHCP server and its prospective clients are on different subnets, appropriate configuration of the network switches or routers will be needed to allow for DHCP relay to occur.
- Try a static IP to verify that the NIC is functioning properly. (Be sure to choose one that is not already in use! Users will be irritated to say the least if an IP used for troubleshooting causes a conflict with the IP of the server. ☺)
- **Advanced users only**: Run WireShark (packet analyzer) on the network to see if DHCP Discovery and Acknowledgement packets are being passed between the nodes.

3.8
Minding the Clock: The Network Time Protocol (NTP)

Time is very important to human beings. Keeping accurate time means not being late for appointments or overlapping scheduled events. In the world of computers, time is equally important, and for similar reasons. First, systems such as email or electronic calendars need both an accurate source of time and the ability to synchronize the time on participating systems (such as the server and its client PCs) so that an appointment set by PC1 for 1 p.m. is seen as such by all others. To accommodate these needs, the Network Time Protocol (NTP)—sometimes called the Simple Network Time Protocol (SNTP)—was created.

3.8.1
A Brief History of Time [Servers][54]

The history of time servers and the Network Time Protocol begins, of all places, in the United States Naval Observatory (USNO), located in Washington, D.C. In 1845, a "time ball" was installed to drop precisely at noon each day, thus providing an accurate measure of time against which citizens could set their timepieces. Ships departing on the Potomac River could also use this as way to synchronize their clocks before putting out to sea, and so would have an accurate beginning to their voyage. Starting in 1865, with the dawn of the telegraph age and the lines laid by Western Union, the Navy began sending out a signal

---

[54]Yes, this title was unabashedly stolen from Stephen Hawking's famous book of the same name (http://www.amazon.com/Brief-History-Time-Stephen-Hawking/dp/0553380168).☺

(the Time Service) to provide an accurate time source for railroads. In the process, the Observatory developed a means of determining longitude by comparing the time reported locally with that of a remote location. By exchanging such information, navigational calculations could be wrought. (Satellites in low-Earth orbit now provide Global Positioning System, a process that also requires an accurate time source and similar calculations derived therefrom).

Over the years that followed, various means were invented to provide a more reliable source of time. Among these was the cesium-beam ("atomic") clock, a version of which was built in 1955 and could maintain time to within plus or minus 1 second every 300 years. Regardless of the underlying technology, the concept was the same: a *master clock* provided a reliable source against which other timepieces could be measured and synchronized. Today, the master clocks maintained by the USNO are housed in a specially-designed vault, and serve as the source for millions of other devices, including…wait for it…*time servers* on the public Internet.

3.8.2
Carpe Momentum ("Seize the Moment")

Like DNS and other systems we've encountered, NTP is a hierarchical topology. A layer within the hierarchy is called by the Latin name *stratum*. *Stratum 0* is thus the root, with additional *strata* (the plural form of *stratum*) following therefrom. The USNO maintains a number of stratum 1 time servers, which derive their time from the master clock (serving as stratum 0). Thus, the top-level servers synchronize with the most accurate means of timekeeping currently available. Nodes that exist at lower strata (for example, stratum 3) synchronize with a server or servers at a higher level (probably stratum 2) on a regular basis. Stratum 1 time servers are available only to designated stratum 2 time servers within their same time zone, or to other servers by special arrangement.

In order to not overload the stratum 1 and 2 servers, end-users and organizations are also encouraged/required to synchronize with lower-level time servers that are geographically close to them. This is the same principle as exists with DNS: an individual user or company would configure systems to contact a DNS server hosted by their Internet provider or other such organization, rather than the root time servers themselves.

By synchronizing with time servers, a group of computers are able to keep time with a higher degree of accuracy than would otherwise be possible. The exact level of this accuracy is dependent on several factors, however, such as the latency of the Internet itself—that is, the speed with which information from Time Server A can reach Time

Server B. Latency is another reason to always synchronize the clock of a given machine with a time server that is geographically close. To simplify this process, the NTP Project, an organization of time-minded individuals and entities (including the USNO) have created a so-called *pool* of time servers against which other computers can be synchronized. Servers participating in the pool are voluntarily added by companies or organizations for the benefit of others, and a website[55] is maintained to disseminate the information needed to make use of these resources.

3.8.3
"Repent, and SYN no more"

Once the connection in the TCP session described above is closed, it can be used for another TCP session. But what if it is not closed, or worse, remains "half-open"? Just such a situation can occur in the case of a form of Denial-of-Service (DoS) attack called a *SYN flood*. A Denial-of-Service attack aims to do what it is called: deny service to legitimate clients of an application or web service. In the case of the SYN flood, the method is both simple and effective. Multiple SYN packets are transmitted at once, "flooding" the target with TCP requests. The SYN-ACK is received from the target, but no ACK is sent in reply. Thus, the connection is left "half-open," tying up resources on the server but accomplishing nothing in the process. When enough of these TCP sessions have built up, all available connections are used up, and the server is rendered unresponsive to legitimate clients.

The Internet community was first alerted to the dangers of SYN flood attacks in 1996. Since that time, various methods for countering this form of DoS have been devised. Modern enterprise and even consumer-grade firewalls now include features that can counter SYN floods and other forms of DoS attacks, making it less of a concern than a decade or so ago.

---

[55] http://www.pool.ntp.org/en

You are here

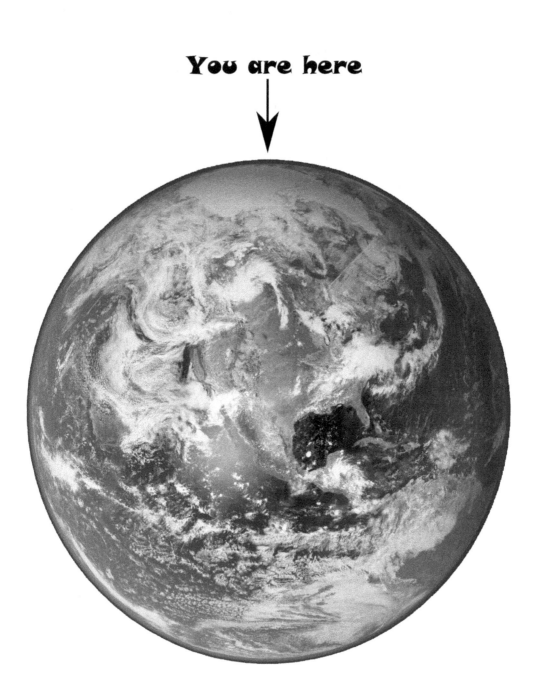

CHAPTER 4:
NETWORKING, THE MICROSOFT WAY

4.1
Windows Peer-to-Peer Networks

All versions of Windows since Windows for Networks (3.1) have been natively capable of participating in networks to one degree or another. The aforementioned operating system was designed to participate in a "workgroup" or *peer-to-peer* network, in which all machines are effectively equal (i.e., there is no designated "server" machine). Peer-to-peer networks are generally small, and do not support the more advanced applications (e.g., Exchange or SQL Server) that require a Windows server operating system in order to be installed.

(30) Peer-to-Peer LAN

The diagram depicts a simple peer-to-peer network, in which a number of Windows workstations are connected to a SOHO firewall/router/switch, which is then connected to the Internet. Note that the printer and router are assigned static IP addresses in a private class C subnet 192.168.1.x/24. Workstations are assigned IPs from DHCP, which in this topology is likely running on the firewall/router, which also forwards DNS queries to a public name server (probably maintained by the ISP). The firewall/router acts as the gateway from the private LAN (192.168.1.x/24) to the public Internet; as such, the *default gateway* for all internal nodes is the internal IP assigned to the firewall, in this case, 192.168.1.1. The outside IP of the firewall is then configured to point to the default gateway of the ISP.

In a workgroup scenario such as is depicted above, one of the PCs might be designated as the "host" for file-serving or other purposes. This does not constitute a "fileserver" in the technical sense of a Windows Server machine, but is usually adequate for small installations. Communication between internal machines will be by NetBIOS broadcast (NetBT).

<h1 style="text-align:center">4.2
Client/Server Topology</h1>

As already mentioned, a Windows network that includes a dedicated machine running a Windows Server is (usually) a client/server topology. The caveat is that if a Windows Server is not configured for a domain, the network would effectively remain a workgroup.

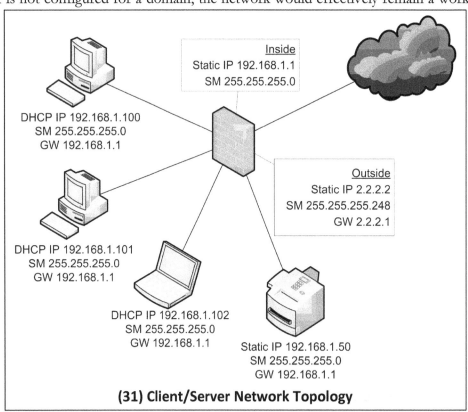

(31) Client/Server Network Topology

82

Assuming this is the case, however, the network operates somewhat differently than a peer-to-peer topology.

The diagram above depicts a small client/server network topology. From a physical standpoint, the only distinction between this and the peer-to-peer network is the introduction of a dedicated server. From a logical standpoint, however, the differences are more fundamental. With the introduction of the Windows Server, the 2nd topology can (and should) be configured as a Windows *domain*. A Windows domain functions in the same way as the Domain Name Space discussed above (see Chapter 1). Using the same hierarchical arrangement, a Windows domain has a root domain and (perhaps) subdomains. NetBIOS names assigned to clients and servers within the domain become the first part of the Fully Qualified Domain Name (FQDN). Starting with Windows 2000, a Windows domain is built upon DNS, and in fact requires a DNS server to be installed in order for the domain to function properly.

4.1.2.1
Who Is In Control?

A machine running the Windows Server operating system is either a Domain Controller (DC) or a Member Server. A Domain Controller contains a copy of the Active Directory (AD) database used for resource management (e.g., access authentication and security). The DC generally also hosts the Domain Name Service (DNS) and/or Dynamic Host Configuration Protocol (DHCP), both of which are used in conjunction with AD for management of nodes and services on the network.[56] Finally, on a Domain Controller can contain the Global Catalog, a higher function of AD that holds information about the Windows domain.

By contrast, a server used to host services or applications such as web, file server, or database are not required to run on a DC. Quite to the contrary, for security purposes, Microsoft recommends that SQL Server and other applications *not* be run on the same machine as Active Directory. Such a machine is referred to simply as a Member Server. What distinguishes this from a workstation is (1) the version of the operating system used, i.e., the "server" version, such as Windows 2008 R2, vs. a desktop edition such as Windows 7; and (2) the services hosted on the machine. For example, it is not common to host web, file server, or database roles on a server that is running Windows 7, at least not for production purposes.

---

[56] Technically, DNS and DHCP can be run on a server that is not configured as a DC. Under most circumstances, however, these services are installed on the same machine as Active Directory.

4.3
NetBIOS:
The (Original) Lifeblood of Windows Networking

The Greek word bios means "life" (hence, *biology* is the study of life). In the context of computer hardware, the BIOS (Basic Input Output System) is specialized software (also called *firmware*) stored on a Read Only Memory (ROM) chip inside the machine. BIOS loads whenever the machine is powered on or rebooted, and is responsible for establishing the initial communication between various peripherals, such as CPU, memory, and storage, which are necessary for the operating system to then load.

Network Basic Input/Output System (NetBIOS) is the name given to a protocol originally developed in the 1980s to allow applications on different computers to communicate over a network. Like its firmware counterpart, NetBIOS was the foundation upon which other software would function, being the means of communication rather than the application data itself. Early versions of Windows used NetBIOS as a means by which computers on the same workgroup could communicate. This was later extended into Microsoft's client/server topology, and remains the foundation for certain functionality in the Windows platform. The implementation of NetBIOS that is used in current and recent version of Windows is encapsulated in IP, and is called—aptly enough—*NetBIOS over TCP/IP.*

4.3.1
The NetBIOS Naming Convention

NetBIOS provides a means for both *session services* and a *naming service*. The NetBIOS name service works in a fashion somewhat like the Domain Name Service (DNS). Each computer is assigned a *name*, which must be unique to the network. These names are then "registered" so that other machines can find it by that name. A *NetBIOS name* is a string 16 bytes (ASCII characters) in length. The first 15 are the for the computer name, which can contain letters and numbers, but not most special characters like punctuation marks or underscores, though dashes are permitted. Computer names shorter than 15 bytes are padded with spaces, while those longer than 15 bytes are truncated. The final (16th) byte designates the service that is being used. This 16th byte is sometimes displayed in hex (e.g., "0x00" is the hex designator for the Workstation service), though more often as the last 2 digits in square brackets. The following are common NetBIOS designations for Windows services:

Server service*COMPUTERNAME* + [20]
Workstation service*COMPUTERNAME* + [00]
Messenger Service*COMPUTERNAME*[03]

In the world of Windows, the *Server* service is commonly called "file and print sharing." The *Workstation* service is the client that connects to a Server service. The Messenger service is a basic peer-to-peer instant messaging service that was popular in earlier versions of Windows. Thus, for common Windows network usage, the Server and Workstation services (and their dependent services) are the most important.

4.3.2
What's In a Name?

NetBIOS differentiates between two types of names: the *exclusive* name and the *group* name. An *exclusive* NetBIOS name is one assigned to a given computer. Conversely, a *group* name designates a collection of multiple computers. Furthermore, Windows allows the NetBIOS name and the DNS hostname of a computer to be the same. Finally, since all current and recent versions of Windows use NetBIOS over TCP/IP as their protocol stack, troubleshooting issues requires understanding how these work together.

4.3.3
NetBIOS Name Resolution

When a computer running NetBIOS is booted, it registers itself on the network by issuing a *broadcast* message. This broadcast is sent to all nodes on the network, and makes the availability of the machine and its NetBIOS applications known to the others. The NetBIOS name that is broadcast must be unique on the network. For example, there can only be one machine with NetBIOS name "PC1" on a given network. If another machine were added to the network with the NetBIOS name "PC1," it would encounter an error when trying to register itself with the other nodes. This is because each machine maintains a cache of known NetBIOS names, and will respond with a negative reply if another machine attempts to register a known name. If there is no conflict, a positive reply is sent, and the new node is "known."

A NetBIOS application on the local host that needs to communicate with a NetBIOS application on another host first passes its request to NetBIOS (Layer 5 or Session layer), which as you might recall from Chapter 1 was described thus:

[Ahem…]

Layer 5 of the OSI model is the Session layer, and functions in an administrative role, being responsible for creating, managing and terminating sessions (requests or responses) transmitted between applications running on separate nodes. For example, computer A is running a copy of a program that requests data from Computer B. It is the Session layer that interprets the request sent from Computer A to Computer B and then replies accordingly. The actual data sent is not handled by this layer, but it provides (in conjunction with layers 1-4) the mechanism by which the data exchange can take place.[57]

Note that the Layer 5 passes its information down to Layers 4 through 1, each of which must do their part to see that the request from PC1 to PC2 is communicated properly. The first step in this process is to associate the NetBIOS name with an IPv4 address.[58] This is because, as you might recall, Windows systems use NetBIOS over TCP/IP. Passing from NetBIOS at Layer 5 to TCP at Layer 4, the control mechanisms are thus put into place (hence the term "Transport Control Mechanism"). Arriving at Layer 3, the Network layer, we come to the heart of the issue: finding the way by which PC1 at IP 1.1.1.2 can find the machine whose IP address is 1.1.1.3. NetBIOS by itself cannot find the other machine, because the NetBIOS protocol is running atop the TCP/IP protocol. To maintain this differentiation, NetBIOS over TCP/IP is referred to as *NetBT*.

Recall that when the network layer (Layer 3) needs to find the IP address of another machine, it may accomplish this by one of three ways: (1) the ARP cache may remember the answer; (2) the *hosts* file may contain the answer; (3) it may query a name server (DNS); (4) if all of these fail, it will issue a broadcast (ARP) to the network and wait for a reply. This process is called *name resolution*.

NBT operates along similar lines. By default, the Windows implementation of NetBT is configured to first check the local NetBT cache (which is different from the ARP cache used by TCP/IP). This is the fastest method, but may not always have the answer, even in a fairly static environment. The reason is that the cache clears itself out after a time (~10 minutes) in order to keep entries from growing "stale" (i.e., out of date). Since stale entries would result in wrong information and delays, this is a good thing; however, the reason for the cache timeout was to limit the amount of RAM (Random Access Memory) used on the system. In the world of desktop machines boasting gigabytes of memory, this seems irrelevant, but one must recall that the NetBIOS protocol was originally designed for computers that had only 640K (or less) of memory! In order to maintain backward

---

[57]And now, gentle reader, you see that all the blathering-on about the OSI model truly laid the foundation for the rest of this study. ☺

[58]Recall that this study is limited to IP Version 4 (IPv4). NetBIOS over TCP/IP can *only* run on IPv4, not IPv6.

compatibility, this limitation was never lifted, so the cache, while still useful, does not operate as efficiently as it might if designed for modern systems in which RAM usage is not as much of an issue.

If no answer is found in cache, NetBT queries a file called *lmhosts*, which like the *hosts* file, contains information about hostnames and IP addresses. In this case, however, the names are not DNS names, but NetBIOS names.[59] It next attempts to contact a NetBIOS Name Server (NBNS). In the world of Microsoft networks, this is handled by the *Windows Internet Naming Service* (WINS). WINS is to NetBIOS what DNS is to domain names: a database containing information that associates a name with an IP address. Like DNS, this information may be replicated to other name servers; unlike DNS, however, there is no hierarchical organization with WINS servers, because NetBIOS is a "flat" topology.

If neither the cache nor lmhosts file nor NBNS query returns the information needed, NetBT resorts to broadcast. NetBIOS traffic has a reputation for being "chatty"; that is, NetBT can easily flood a network with traffic that is nothing but broadcasts of one machine trying to find another machine. One solution to this problem is to configure one or more WINS servers, which then answer NetBIOS queries for the network. This precludes the need for broadcasts that rely on the workstations to respond individually.

4.3.4
NetBIOS Node Types

A *node type* specifies how a NetBIOS client will interact with the network. For our purposes, two node types are important: *B-node (broadcast)* and *H-node (hybrid)*. As the name infers, a B-node uses broadcast only to resolve NetBIOS names. That is, if the local cache does not possess the answer, NetBT broadcasts are used to find the remote host. This is the method for a peer-to-peer network that lacks a NetBIOS name server (NBNS). Since the NBNS of choice for Microsoft networks is WINS, and since WINS runs on the Windows Server operating system, it is a safe bet that a network that does not have an NBNS does not have a Windows Server running WINS, and is therefore not on a domain; hence, it is a peer-to-peer network.

The distinction between a B-node and H-node is applicable for both a "server" *and* "client" or workstation machine. Whether or not they use broadcast or WINS depends on the network setup; a machine configured with entries in the WINS setup screens (and thus expecting to receive answers to queries from an NBNS) uses hybrid mode, while one

---

[59]This distinction is blurred by the fact that Windows uses the names interchangeably. Technically, it would be possible to assign a machine a NetBIOS name that does not correspond to its DNS hostname.

without these settings uses broadcast mode. Finally, if a node using hybrid mode fails to get a response from a name server (WINS), it resorts to broadcast to resolve the NetBIOS name in question. Thus, if WINS is absent, misconfigured, or malfunctioning, the result can be a more "chatty" network in which the various machines communicate via broadcast rather than unicast NBNS query. This, in turn, can cause degradation of network response for other applications, and end-user displeasure.

4.3.5
NetBIOS Limitations

By default, NetBIOS cannot traverse routers or firewalls, so broadcasts are limited to the local network only.[60] If hosts on different networks (separated by a router or firewall) require NetBIOS or NetBT traffic to pass between them, this must be accomplished through alternate means, such as WINS or the LMHOSTS file, which will always have the "answer" to the NetBIOS queries from either side.

4.4
TCP/IP:
The (Other) Lifeblood of Windows Networking

The implementation of TCP/IP on the Windows platform is in many ways consistent with that of other platforms, such as Linux or UNIX. The differences, of course, lie in the means by which changes are made, and the location of certain configuration files. Finally, for those who may have previous experience with different versions of Windows, the next point will be well-made: Microsoft tends to change the settings from version to version, and so documenting each is difficult. The following discussion will be limited to an overview of the theory and practice, but sparing in minutiae that can be found elsewhere.[61]

---

[60]A feature called *NetBIOS broadcast forwarding* is available on some network devices, but its use is highly discouraged. NetBIOS is known *not* to function over the public Internet.

[61]As with almost everything these days, Google is a goldmine of information. With respect to this section, the differences in network configuration screens, locations of icons, etc., between different versions of Windows (e.g., XP vs. Vista or Windows 7) make documenting all of this tedious and redundant. Myriad external resources exist on the specifics of each OS.

4.4.1
To DHCP, or Not to DHCP? (That Is the Query)

The first step in connecting a Windows machine (client or server) to the network is assignment of an IP address. This is done in one of 2 ways: statically (manual entry) or dynamically via DHCP. In most cases, servers and other network peripherals (printers, copiers, network storage devices) are assigned a static IP. This is because these are fixed resources that must be easily found on the network. A static IP ensures that unintended changes are not made to the network configuration that would render the resource unavailable. Conversely, it is common practice to use DHCP for workstations and other devices that may move around or for which a fixed configuration is not necessary. For example, as long as a user can access the fileserver, it does not matter whether the laptop or desktop he or she uses has a static or dynamic IP. By using dynamic IPs, however, the network administrator can more easily replace a faulty machine or NIC and quickly get the machine back up and running.

Configuration of the IP address and related information is done through the GUI, as shown below in the following screenshots from my Windows 7 machine. The first step is to get to the Local Area Connection screen.

On Windows XP or Server 2000/2003, this is in the **Control Panel→Network and Internet Connections** (new view) or **Control Panel→Network Connections** (classic view). On Windows Vista, Windows 7, and Server 2008, it is under **Control Panel→Network and Internet→Network and Sharing Center**.

Click the **Properties** button and the next screen appears. Click to highlight **Internet Protocol Version 4** and click **Properties**.

If the machine is to have a static IP, the address and subnet mask must also be entered. Recall from Chapters 1 and 2 that were this an isolated network, unconnected to the Internet, a default gateway would not be needed, since no other networks would be available. Likewise, DNS entries may or may not be needed, though for a computer that has a default gateway, DNS entries will most likely be required in order to resolve URL or hostnames to IP addresses when browsing the Internet.

(32) Local Area Connection Status

(33) TCP/IP Properties

4.4.2
Name Resolution with HOSTS and DNS

The HOSTS file on a Windows system can be found in the following folder: *%SYSTEMROOT%\System32\drivers\etc\hosts*. There are several things to note. First, *%SYSTEMROOT%* designates the directory in which Windows is installed. By default, for Windows NT and Windows 2000 systems, this is *C:\WINNT*. For all others, it is *C:\Windows*. Secondly, the HOSTS file is a simple text file with no file extension; this is a tie-in to its roots in the world of UNIX, which does not require file extensions. To open the file, simply point Notepad, Wordpad, or another text editor to the file. Finally, on Windows Vista, Windows 7, and Windows Server 2008, it is necessary to open the text editor with elevated credentials in order to save any changes made to the file. To do this, right-click on the Notepad icon (found under **Start→All Programs→Accessories**) and choose **Run as Administrator**.

As noted above, common practice is to use DHCP to assign IP addresses to workstations. Among the settings configured by DHCP is option to specify the DNS server(s) to be queried for name resolution. Since most small networks utilize a SOHO router/firewall with DHCP server capabilities built-in, this device becomes the DHCP server for that network. Moreover, this device commonly derives its own external IP address from a DHCP server maintained by the ISP. This information is then shared with internal clients, and configured as part of the private DHCP scope to point their queries to one or more external (public) DNS servers.

If neither DNS nor the HOSTS file is configured with the answer to a query, the hostname cannot be resolved to an IP. Address Resolution Protocol (ARP) is still used at Layer 2, however, to resolve the IP to a MAC address. Thus, an IP application running on this network would need to know the IP address of the remote system, since the hostname would not be resolvable.

4.4.3
The "No-Win Scenario"

In the world of *Star Trek*, Starfleet Academy cadets were put through a training scenario called the "Kobayashi Maru." The point of the exercise was to test the character of a commander facing a the dreaded "no-win scenario."

A real-world example of a no-win scenario involves a workstation on a Windows domain for which DNS is either not configured, misconfigured, or malfunctioning. Upon boot, the workstation queries DNS to locate the domain controller on the network. In the process, it is looking for the SRV record that corresponds to the identity of the domain controller. If this query goes unanswered, the system retries again and again until it finally times-out. At this point, the system switches to NBT broadcasts and (should) receive a response from the domain controller (assuming the server is running NBT). Having resolved the name of the server to an IP address, it is then able to issue the Kerberos commands to login to the network.

4.5
Windows Command-Line Tools for TCP/IP

As you delve further into the Windows operating system, especially the server or enterprise desktop versions, you discover that "Yes, Virginia, there is a command-line" (that's CLI for those who crave more acronyms).) In fact, Windows is increasingly-dependent on CLI for administrative functions of various products, including Windows Server and Exchange 2007/2010. And of course, there is PowerShell, which is a topic unto itself.

The Windows command-line tools for TCP/IP and NetBT are helpful for both troubleshooting and routine information gathering purposes. Several of the most "popular" are listed here. Many more exist within the operating system. The reader is encouraged to view the help screens for command syntax, and the *Fundamentals* document for more in-depth coverage.

4.5.1
ping

Of all the tools available, the **ping** command is perhaps the most popular. The concept of a "ping" derives from sonar. A ship or submarine broadcasts a short ultrasonic burst, then waits to hear the echo that follows. By measuring the time it takes for the echo to be received, the distance between the two vessels can be calculated, since the speed of sound through water is a known constant.

In computer networking, the ping command sends an *Internet Control Message Protocol* (ICMP) packet (Layer 2) with the destination IP or hostname of a remote system. (Using a

```
C:\>ping www.google.com

Pinging www.google.com [74.125.225.244] with 32 bytes of data:
Reply from 74.125.225.244: bytes=32 time=172ms TTL=55
Reply from 74.125.225.244: bytes=32 time=93ms TTL=55
Reply from 74.125.225.244: bytes=32 time=121ms TTL=55
Reply from 74.125.225.244: bytes=32 time=136ms TTL=55

Ping statistics for 74.125.225.244:
    Packets: Sent = 4, Received = 4, Lost = 0 (0% loss),
Approximate round trip times in milli-seconds:
    Minimum = 93ms, Maximum = 172ms, Average = 130ms
```

(34) The *ping* Command

hostname assumes that DNS or HOSTS is configured properly, and that the hostname is thereby resolvable.) It then waits for the echo-reply message to be sent back. Ping and ICMP can be helpful to determine that a node is "alive," i.e., that it is functioning at a basic network level. Note, however, that a ping response does not mean the higher-level application protocols are functioning properly, nor that the node in question is doing all it should be. Ping only proves that the network connectivity at Layer 2 is working. Note also that ICMP can be blocked by firewalls to protect against port scanning attacks, and so may not reply at all, even when the remote node is functioning fine.

4.5.2
tracert (trace route)

Like ping, the **tracert** command uses ICMP packets, but instead of a single series of broadcasts, multiple pings are sent to each "hop" along the route. As each is returned, the time is calculated in milliseconds (ms), giving a measure of how far and how many routers lie between a source and destination node. Trace route is helpful when troubleshooting Internet issues.

```
C:\>tracert www.google.com

Tracing route to www.google.com [74.125.227.115]
over a maximum of 30 hops:

  1     7 ms     7 ms     7 ms  192.168.1.1
  2    13 ms    15 ms    15 ms  10.107.128.1
  3    18 ms    13 ms    21 ms  68.13.10.141
  4   128 ms   136 ms   142 ms  68.13.9.241
  5    43 ms    34 ms    35 ms  mtc1dsrj02-ae3.0.rd.om.cox.net [68.13.14.13]
  6    51 ms    45 ms    36 ms  68.1.5.140
  7    35 ms    29 ms    29 ms  72.14.212.233
  8   237 ms   202 ms   216 ms  72.14.233.65
  9    36 ms    30 ms    31 ms  209.85.240.91
 10   269 ms   285 ms   296 ms  dfw06s16-in-f19.1e100.net [74.125.227.115]

Trace complete.
```

(35) The *tracert* (traceroute) command

4.5.3
nslookup (Nameserver lookup)

The **nslookup** command is a simple command-line client for querying a DNS server. Nslookup can be configured to query either the default server (as configured in the network settings manually or via DHCP), or a specific DNS server. For example, a Windows machine may be unable to resolve the hostname server1.xyz.com from the browser or command-line. When using nslookup, however, the query is run not against local cache or local DNS, but against a known public DNS server. This machine returns the correct answer, so the problem is local. The next step would be to clear local DNS cache and/or check local

```
C:\>nslookup
Default Server:  cdns2.cox.net
Address:  68.105.28.12

> google.com
Server:  cdns2.cox.net
Address:  68.105.28.12

Non-authoritative answer:
Name:      google.com.mccnet.mccneb.edu
Address:   72.215.225.9
```

(36) The *nslookup* Command

local DNS to see if the record is stale or even non-existent.

Recall that caching occurs on the DNS server as well as the local workstation, so cache at both locations should be cleared. This should force the system to query the public DNS server and retrieve an accurate record in response.

4.5.4
ipconfig

The command-line tool for extracting information related to the TCP/IP configuration of a Windows machine is *ipconfig*. The command **ipconfig** returns basic information, while **ipconfig /all** gives more detailed information. Specifically, but using the **/all** switch, information on the configuration of DHCP, DNS, WINS, and so forth, is returned.

Note the amount of information available from this single screen. In my opinion, using the **ipconfig** commands is preferable to the graphical interface, in that much more information can be gleaned from a single output, rather than bouncing between different screens of the GUI. But aside from simple information-gathering, the **ipconfig** command provides the means for release and renewal of an IP address that has been assigned via DHCP, clearing the local DNS cache, or registering the local machine with the default DNS server. For help, type **ipconfig /?** at the command prompt.

Note that on Windows Vista and higher, the TCP/IP commands take into account 2 different sets of syntax, one related to IPv4 and the other to IPv6. Only those related to IPv4 will be discussed here. The **ipconfig/release** and **ipconfig/renew** commands work together, and are only applicable to a machine to which an IP has been assigned by a DHCP server. The **/release** command does 2 things. First, it releases the IP from the local NIC to which it had been assigned. This also severs any network connectivity, leaving the client disconnected from any network resources. The **/release** command also sends a signal to the DHCP server with which the client was registered of its intention to no longer use the IP in question.

The **ipconfig/renew** command, conversely, sends a message to the DHCP requesting assignment of a new IP. In many cases, this will be the same IP that was just released. This is because the DHCP server assign IPs in numerical order. Assuming no other node requested an IP in the interim (i.e., between the issuance of the **ipconfig/release** and **ipconfig/renew** commands), the IP just released is now available, and thus will be reissued to the (same) node.

The **ipconfig/flushdns** command is used to clear the local DNS cache. For example, when a user opens a web browser and enters an address, the system does a lookup against DNS to find the IP address that corresponds to that site or hostname. Once retrieved, the answer is stored for reuse. This allows the system to more quickly respond the next time that address is requested, since the answer is "known ." If the cache is outdated or stale, however, the "known" answer might be *wrong*. The **ipconfig/flushdns** command therefore provides a means of clearing the cache and forcing the machine to query a DNS server, which (presumably) has the correct information.

4.5.5
Who dat, netstat?

The **netstat** command gives a view into the connections and listening ports on the local machine. A good use for this command is to see if "unauthorized" applications residing on the machine are making or accepting network connections. Such a situation may indicate the presence of a Trojan or spyware program. The utility allows for various options, all of which are listed with descriptions in the help screen, available by typing the following: **netstat /?**

When used with **–a** switch, **netstat** outputs a list of all current connections and listening ports. When used with the **–b** switch, the output changes to the executables (program filenames) that are establishing the connections. Bear in mind that this is a static list (point-in-time). In order to "refresh" the list, the command must be reissued. Thus, to monitor a system over a period of time, **netstat** is not the optimal tool; a better option would be a so-called "packet sniffer."[62] When troubleshooting suspected network issues, it may be helpful to use **netstat –e** (Ethernet statistics), which lists information related to the network layer. The **–s** switch then adds per-protocol information.

4.5.6
nbtstat

The **nbtstat** command is used to troubleshoot NetBT on Windows systems. For example, **nbtstat -r** lists the names of machines resolved and/or registered through NetBIOS. Separate listings are given for other Windows machines discovered through broadcast, vs. those found by WINS lookup.

---

[62]A number of complex (and some quit expensive) commercial *packet sniffers* exist. The most popular freely-available one, which is also feature-rich, is WireShark (http://www.wireshark.org). WireShark runs on Windows, MacOS, and a number of Linux and UNIX systems. For a Windows-only solution, Microsoft offers Network Monitor:

http://www.microsoft.com/downloads/en/details.aspx?FamilyID=983b941d-06cb-4658-b7f6-3088333d062f&displaylang=en.

4.5.7
net view

Finally, we come to the **net view** command, which provides information about the network configuration of the Windows machines found on the LAN. Note that the options available are contingent on the type of network, such as workgroup (peer-to-peer) vs. a Windows domain. The **net view /workgroup:[workgroup name]** lists all computers known to the master browser. (Note that this command does not work if the machine is a member of a domain.) The **net view /domain:[domain name]** command lists all computers known to a *domain master browser*. Finally, **net view /cache** lists computers held in the local computer browser cache.

CHAPTER 5:
WINDOWS® FILE AND PRINT SHARING

5.1
Share and Share Alike

The desktop (Windows XP, Vista, 7) and Server editions of Windows can function as a file- or print-server to other nodes on the network. That is, PC2 can "share" a file or entire folder to the network. This functionality is controlled by the Server service that is part of NetBIOS over TCP/IP (NetBT). File and folder permissions on the machine restrict who (i.e., what username) can connect to and read/write/change/delete the files on the share. The remote machine accesses this share by pointing to a pathname called the *Universal Naming Convention* (UNC, also called the Uniform Naming Convention). The syntax of a UNC includes the server (NetBIOS name) and folder share name, separated by backslashes. The UNC begins with a double backslash; all other units are separated by single backslash, as shown here:

\\servername\sharename

Thus, the UNC \\Server01\Data would point to a share name called *Documents* on the machine whose NetBIOS name is *Server01*. *Data* is the "share name," or virtual directory name by which the folder is known to the network, and as such, is not necessarily identical to the folder on the host machine.

In this example, we see that C:\Data is shared as \\Server01\Data, but what if there were two different Data folders, one at the root of the drive (C:\) and the other somewhere

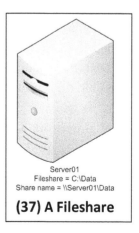

Server01
Fileshare = C:\Data
Share name = \\Server01\Data

(37) A Fileshare

else? Share names must be unique, so if both of these folders are to be shared on the network, a different naming convention must be found. Thus, what appears as \\Server01\Data could actually point to a different volume on the host, such as C:\stuff\Documents. Either way, remote machines accessing the share would see the documents presented by that share, provided the user had appropriate permissions.

The mechanics of Windows File and Print Sharing take bring us to a discussion of NetBIOS over TCP/IP (NetBT), which we have seen before, and 2 other protocol which we have not yet encountered: the Common Internet File System (CIFS) and the Server Message Block (SMB).

5.2
Something Old, Something New: NetBT

NetBT (NetBIOS over TCP/IP) is the foundation upon which Windows file and print sharing functions. As noted in Chapter 4, the earliest versions of Windows used NetBIOS as the Layer 3 protocol running atop an Ethernet network (Layer 2). NetBIOS had been developed as an Application Programming Interface (API) for IBM's own PC-Network LAN technology. In its original form, NetBIOS was limited to at most 80 nodes on the network (quite small by today's standards). When IBM later changed to a different physical network topology called Token Ring (against which Ethernet would eventually win out as rival technology), an emulator was created to allow earlier systems to integrate with the new network infrastructure. The emulator, named NetBIOS Extended User Interface (NetBEUI), extended NetBIOS to support the higher numbers of nodes that Token Ring offered. At the same time, Microsoft developed its own NetBIOS implementation, which it also named NetBEUI, but which was in fact a completely different protocol. Though the IBM original was lost in the sands of time, the name continued within the Microsoft realm. The first version of Windows to support networking, Windows for Workgroups (v3.11), used NetBEUI as its underlying protocol. This remained the case for Windows 9x and NT, and as late as Windows XP, NetBEUI was an optional (though unsupported) protocol for networking computers together. Thus, it is still possible on a Windows XP to build an Ethernet network using NetBEUI rather than TCP/IP as its Layer 3 protocol, though without IP, the system cannot communicate with most other network devices or access the Internet.[63]

---

[63] Why one would do this is questionable at best, however. As posted on Microsoft's support website: "Support for the NetBEUI network protocol has been discontinued in Windows XP. This protocol is not available to install in Windows XP. The NetBEUI protocol was developed in

The year 1987 brought a change of tide with the publication of a standard by which NetBIOS could be encapsulated within IP. This meant that computers running applications that used NetBIOS as their protocol, but which needed to communicate with the Internet or other devices running IP, could do so in a more seamless way. The result was NetBIOS over TCP/IP, abbreviated either NetBT or NBT. All versions of Windows now use NetBT to support backward compatibility for applications that require NetBIOS, among them, the services that provide file and print sharing.

5.2.1
Service With a Smile

In order for file and print sharing to function properly on a network, several services must be active and their respective ports able to communicate between nodes. The first is the NetBIOS Name Service (*netbios-ns*) which operates on UDP port 137. The second is the NetBIOS Datagram (*netbios-dgm*) service, which operates on UDP port 138, and facilitates communication between NetBIOS applications running on separate network devices. Third is the NetBIOS Session service (*netbios-ssn*)—commonly called the *Server* service in Windows—which operates over TCP port 139. This service runs on all versions of Windows, and is the service that allows network sharing of files, folders, and printers. In short, for a share to function properly, this service must be running on the machine, and the TCP port 139 open for inbound traffic. Finally, the TCP/IP NetBIOS Helper Service must be running in the background in order for File and Print sharing to function properly. Altogether, Windows File and Print services requires that TCP and UDP ports 135-139 be open for inbound connection to whatever machine is to provide file or print sharing services to the network.

To summarize, the File and Print Sharing capabilities of Windows is inherently built into all current and recent versions of the operating system. This means that whether the nodes participate in a peer-to-peer configuration or a Windows domain, each node could be used to share files and printers across the network.

1985. It is used by network operating systems such as Microsoft LAN Manager, Microsoft Windows for Workgroups, Microsoft Windows 95, and Microsoft Windows NT. The NetBEUI protocol implements the OSI LLC2 protocol, and is a non-routable protocol." See http://support.microsoft.com/kb/306059).

In other words, modern computers that wish to reach the Internet require IP, which is also the foundation for Microsoft's current NetBIOS iteration (NetBIOS over TCP/IP, or NetBT). Since that protocol also allows internal systems to communicate, having NetBEUI installed on a Windows XP system is at best nostalgic, at worst, a waste of time. ☺

5.3
Get Down With SMB? (Yeah, You Know Me!)

As outlined above, NetBIOS is the network layer protocol for Windows file and print sharing. Its application-layer counterpart is Server Message Block (SMB), also called the Common Internet File System (CIFS). SMB is the upper-level protocol that sits atop Ethernet and IP and controls access to network shares as offered by a Windows system. By default, the services described above are enabled and active. Again, a bit of history is in order. Prior to Windows 2000, the SMB protocol ran atop NetBIOS or NetBEUI. Starting with Windows 2000, however, SMB was changed to support operation directly atop TCP/IP. This configuration, known as "direct host SMB," allows the SMB protocol to listen on TCP 445 rather than the NetBIOS ports (UDP 137/138 and TCP 139).

Windows versions prior to Vista use SMB 1.0. SMB 2.0 was introduced with Vista and Server 2008. The new version had a simplified command set to make the protocol less "chatty." The release of Windows 7 and Windows Server 2008 R2 then brought SMB 2.1. To maintain compatibility, newer platforms run both SMB versions, and "negotiate" which to use with a given peer. (This does not always work as designed, and so it is possible to disable SMB 2.x via the registry.)

5.3.1
SMB over NetBT vs. SMB over TCP/IP

All version of Windows later than NT (i.e., Windows 200x, Vista, 7) are capable of running SMB over TCP/IP natively. To change this setting, open the Control Panel and go to Network Connections (Windows 2000/2003/XP) or Network and Sharing Center (Windows Vista/7/2008) and open the properties screen for the Local Area Connection and open aathe Properties screen of the TCP/IP Protocol. In the Advanced section, under the WINS tab, is a section that controls whether or when NetBT is enabled.[64]

A system running Windows 2000 or higher that is configured for NetBT will listen for inbound SMB connections on both the original ports (137/138 UDP and 139 TCP) and the newer port, TCP 445. If a connection is sensed on TCP 445, a reset command is sent to the other ports, and communication is continued on 445. Otherwise, communication continues as on earlier versions of Windows with NetBT. If NetBT is disabled, SMB listens only on TCP 445. This means that a client running a version of Windows prior to

---

[64] It would also be possible to apply this setting to all computers on a Windows domain through use of a Group Policy Object (GPO).

Windows 2000 (NT or 9x, for example) would be unable to communicate with the server machine, because it cannot communicate over the newer SMB over TCP/IP protocol, NetBT being unavailable.

In theory, a network running Windows 200x or higher could disable NetBT altogether and simply rely on SMB over TCP 445 to provide file and print functionality. Nonetheless, even on Windows 7, to ensure backward compatibility, Microsoft conservatively set the default setting in Windows to *enable* NetBT. In practice, changing this should be done only after confirming that other applications that rely on NetBIOS are not present on the network. Since this would require extensive knowledge of the network architecture of every program used by every user, it is probably wisest to leave well enough alone, unless a case can be built that NetBT is producing negative results on the network.

5.3.2
Disabling SMB 2.0

In "mixed" environments it is sometimes necessary to disable SMB 2.0 on those machines running the newer versions of Windows, in order to avoid unnecessary issues that can arise from this backward compatibility. In short, though the Vista/2008/7 machine *should* automatically negotiate the proper protocol with its older peers, this does not always work as intended. In order to alleviate this problem, it is possible to disable SMB 2.0 on a system that is acting as the "client" for another machine. The following commands are required:

```
sc config lanmanworkstation depend= bowser/mrxsmb10/nsi
sc config mrxsmb20 start= disabled
```

To re-enable SMB 2.0 on the "client" machine, use the following commands:

```
sc config lanmanworkstation depend= bowser/mrxsmb10/mrxsmb20/nsi
sc config mrxsmb20 start= auto
```

For a system that is acting as the "server" for another machine, disabling SMB 2.0 requires a change to the registry, instructions for which can be found in the "Workaround" section of the following Microsoft Support article:

http://support.microsoft.com/kb/950836.

The new registry entry instructs Windows to enable or disable SMB 2.0 depending on the setting of this registry entry. A decimal value of 0 (zero) means "disable SMB 2.0," while a decimal value of 1 enables the protocol. Note that changes to this value or key require a system reboot.

5.3.3
When Opportunity Locks

Opportunistic locking, or "Oplocks," is a feature of SMB on various Windows Server and desktop operating system versions that allows a client to "lock" and locally cache data without the risk of another user changing the file. Under normal circumstances, this is a good thing: one does not, for example, want User1 to open a Word document in read/write mode and then allow another user to do the same simultaneously. Furthermore, by locally caching this file, the computer at User1's desk can process information faster and provide better response.

An issue can arise in the case of a shared database file, however, such as an Access or other flat-file database architecture that is not well-suited for large numbers of concurrent client connections. In these cases, it is sometimes necessary to disable Oplocks. Note, however, that this is possible for SMB 1.0. SMB 2.x does not allow Oplocks to be disabled; moreover, if Oplocks are disabled, the "offline files" feature of Windows Vista and 7 fails.[65]

5.4
SMB From the User Perspective

All the technical gibberish aside, end-users interact with the SMB protocol every day, never knowing the complexity that lies beneath. At its simplest, the SMB protocol is merely a means by which a user from one system (such as a workstation) connects to an makes use of a file on a remote system, such as a fileserver.

---

[65]See also http://support.microsoft.com/kb/296264.

5.4.1
The Universal Naming Convention (UNC)

In the world of Windows file sharing, the Universal Naming Convention (UNC; also called the Uniform Naming Convention) designates a path by which a folder (directory) and its contents are accessed across the network. For example, if a folder called Stuff is shared from the server called Server01, the UNC for the fileshare would be \\Server01\Stuff. Note that when I type this in Word, it recognizes this as a UNC, and automatically creates a hyperlink. By clicking the link, a user would be able to browse to the share (if it existed. ☺)

5.4.2
Drive Mapping

A drive mapping assigns a drive letter to a file share, thus pointing a local drive letter (such as S:) to a UNC (such as \\Server01\Stuff). As a result, were a user frequently access files or folders on the share, he or she could simply point Windows Explorer to the S: drive, rather than having to remember the UNC each time.

5.5
Folder Permissions vs. Share Permissions

NTFS permissions are assigned to both the folder or files and the folder share. Depending on the version of Windows involved, a newly-created share may have Everyone set to read-only or full control. It is usually advisable to set more stringent security, specifying users or groups, and then removing the Everyone permission. Otherwise, any system that can access the network could browse the share. Be aware that the same rules about read,. write, and delete apply to shares and to folders, but that these are set and maintained independently.

Suppose, for example, that an administrator creates a folder called C:\Stuff on a computer named SERVER. To the local user of the machine, files can be access through the file system at C:\Stuff. In an attempt to lockdown security, the admin further sets permissions on the C:\Stuff folder to "Authenticated Users" with Full Control granted to that group. Once this change is saved, the default "Everyone" group is removed.

The admin now creates a share pointing to C:\Stuff and names this "Stuff" for the sake of simplicity. The share is accessed via the network at \\SERVER\Stuff. Not realizing it, however, the administrator leaves the default setting of group Everyone with read-only permissions.

Now things get interested. When a user browses tot his share and attempts to open a file, all is well. When that user tries to save changes to the file or create new file or folder, however, a message appears that permission is denied. The admin checks the folder permissions on C:\Stuff and sees that the user (who is a member of Authenticated Users by default) should have read/write permissions. Checking further, however, will show that while the folder permissions are read/write, the share permissions are read-only. The solution is to change the share permissions accordingly.

The moral of the story is this: when configuring fileshares, be sure to set permission on the share and the folder/file. Configuration of one does not affect the other, for they are not linked. This has advantages for the sake of flexibility, but can be confusing when trying to troubleshoot access issues.

5.6
Firewalls and SMB: A Lesson in Conflict Resolution

The combination of firewalls and SMB can be a blessing or a curse, depending on the context. It is always prudent to block all inbound traffic at the perimeter of the network (i.e., the firewall between the private LAN and the Internet. Even SOHO firewalls do this by default, and so afford a level of protection without the user needing to understand the how or why. In this case, SMB ports are also blocked, thus keeping would-be attackers out of your Windows shares.

With respect to internal systems, however, the situation becomes a bit more complicated. Since the release of Windows XP SP2, Microsoft has *enabled* its (in)famous Windows Firewall application by default. As a result, inbound traffic on virtually all ports is blocked, including the ones used by SMB. While it is possible (and even easy) to enable an exception rule for file and print sharing, this is a step that must be undertaken manually (or automated through Group Policy, if available) for each machine on the network that wishes to share files out to the network. The reaction on the part of most users is to simply disable the Windows Firewall altogether, thus alleviating the problem. On a trusted system, this is an option. In larger environments, however, it may leave the system exposed to attack.

The lesson to be learned is to know the context. Weigh the needs of users for quick and painless access to network resources against the implications of a security "free-for-all," and you will find the answer that fits best. Especially for those applications that rely on NetBIOS, however, the answer may be to disable the firewall, or at least ensure that exceptions for SMB work as intended, so connectivity is consistent and usable.

5.7
Designing for Security: Wired vs. Wireless LANs

While wireless networks are outside the main thrust of this study, a quick note is in order with regard to their popularity. With the proliferation of wireless networks (or, more accurately, SOHO router/firewall devices that provide both wired and wireless LAN (WLAN) functionality), it is not uncommon for users to have a mixed environment in which desktop PCs are connected via wired Ethernet, but laptops or other mobile devices connect wirelessly. With respect to security, it is important to note that *most* (if not all) of the SOHO devices with which this author has come into contact draw no boundary between the wired and wireless clients that are attached to the network.

Take, for example, the following topology:

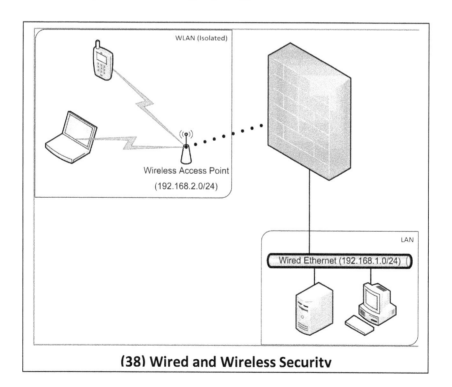

(38) Wired and Wireless Security

Users of the desktop PCs connect via wired 10/100 Ethernet into the SOHO device, which includes a small switch. At the same time, a user with a laptop connects to the wireless access point embedded into the SOHO device, and another user whose

"Smartphone" also has wireless LAN capabilities connects as well.[66] Within this environment, users connected via either method can see each other on the LAN, for the nodes constitute a single segment and subnet. This means that nefarious outsiders seeking access to company resources on one of the machines need only attach to the wireless LAN and then begin poking around until they find something worth a more serious hacking attempt.

The obvious answer is to configure the WLAN with the strongest available encryption. Depending on the security sensitivity of the organization and the technical prowess available, it might also be prudent to use software firewalls on each host to control the flow of traffic into them. Finally, as a more drastic measure, if wireless LAN capabilities are not really needed, it might be prudent to disable them.

---

[66] The designation "802.11b/g/n WLAN" listed under the laptop and Smartphone denote that the devices are using the standard wireless LAN as published by the IEEE.

CHAPTER 6:
THE COMPUTER BROWSER SERVICE

A service called *Computer Browser* is enabled by default on all versions of Windows. It is *Computer Browser* service that obtains, collects, and distributes *browse lists*, or NetBIOS-related information about other computers on the network. In the case of a standalone computer, the browse service runs but has no real value; only when networked with other Windows machines can the Computer Browse service do what it was intended to do: identify and allow access to other NetBIOS-enabled Windows systems on a LAN. This information is stored in a browse list and made accessible to an end-user through the Network[67] graphical interface or via command-line with the **net view** command.

6.1
Browse Service Roles

A Windows computer can hold one of five different roles, as defined below.

---

[67] The list of computers listed in this Graphical User Interface (GUI) is named variously on different versions of Windows. Early versions called it *Network Neighborhood*; this was subsequently changed to *My Network Places*, and in recent versions of Windows, has been shortened to *Network*. Regardless the designation, the function is the same: a listing of NetBIOS computer and/or workgroup names as identified by the Computer Browser service.

6.1.1
Non-browser: The Bashful Loner

The computer browser service is enabled by default. When disabled, the computer becomes a *non-browser*, in the sense that it cannot interact with other NetBIOS systems, nor access the shares they may offer as network resources. In terms of Windows file and print sharing, this machine is "isolated," though it may still interoperate via other protocols.

6.1.2
Potential Browser: The Eager Beaver

A *potential browser* is the polar opposite of the non-browser. With the computer browse service enabled and working, this machine is able to maintain a browse list and is therefore eligible to hold one of the other available roles. Most computers fall into this category, as the browser service is enabled by default.

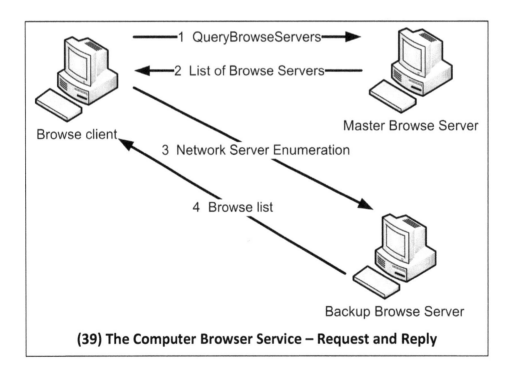

(39) The Computer Browser Service – Request and Reply

6.1.3
Master Browse Server: First Among Equals

A *master browse server* collects the information needed to produce the browse list, and makes this available to other machines on the network. Which computer on the subnet is to hold this role is determined by a process called *election*. (More on this will follow below.)

6.1.4
Backup Browse Server: The Plucky Sidekick

A *backup browse server* holds a copy of the browse list created by the *master browse server*. This information is distributed upon to other machines in the workgroup or domain. Windows Server 2003 domain controllers always hold the role of master browser or backup browser server.

6.1.5
Domain Master Browse Server: Lord of NetBIOS

A *domain master browse server* exists only in a Windows domain topology, and is held on one of the domain controllers. Like the *master browse server* in the Workgroup topology, this machine maintains the browse list for the machines on its same subnet. However, it also maintains a browse list for other subnets, and so is the master browse server not only for its own subnet but the entire domain. Recall that NetBIOS broadcasts cannot traverse a router; thus, all NetBIOS broadcasts are limited to a given subnet. Each subnet therefore has its own Master Browser. These subnet-level browse servers then replicate their data with the Domain Master Browse Server to provide information across the domain, regardless of the subnet.

6.2
Welcome to the (Network) Neighborhood

When the browse service starts, it broadcasts its existence to other nodes in the network. These *browser announcements* follow again after 4 minutes, 8 minutes, and 12 minutes, respectively, and every 12 minutes thereafter. Thus, within 12 minutes or so, the computer acting as master browser should have added an entry into the browse list for this new node. The process of adding this entry is called *registration*. With the initial registration complete, updates are sent via unicast (rather than broadcast), thus ensuring more reliable delivery of browse list updates.

At the same time as registrations are occurring, replication between master browsers and domain master browsers is occurring every 12 minutes. Thus, at least one 12-minute cycle will have passed before the domain master browser receives notification from the master browser that a new NetBIOS name has been registered. Since propagation always occurs on this 12-minute cycle, other machines will be notified as well, but those on remote subnets might take a number of cycles. Depending on the number of subnets involved and the routes between them, this means that total propagation of the browse list to account for a new node will be some multiple of 12 minutes.

6.3
Digital Democracy:
The Master Browse Server Election

The determination of which Potential Browser becomes Master or Backup Browse Server is made by a process called *election*. Any computer holding the role of Potential browser, Master Browse Server, Backup Browse Server, or Domain Master Browse Server can initiate an election by broadcasting a *Request Election* message. When another browse client receives this message, it examines it to determine whether or not it can become the master browse server. This process involves specific rules based on *ranking*.

6.3.1
First Among Equals

"All the browse servers are equal, but some are more equal than others."

Each browse client is assigned a *ranking*. It is this ranking that is compared to the information contained in the Request Election broadcast and used to determine the outcome of the election. In this sense, the election is actually rigged: a client that receives a Request Election message from a machine of *lower* rank than its own broadcasts its own Request Election message and enters an *Election In Progress* state. Conversely, a client that receive a Request Election message of *higher* rank than its own simply requests to know which machine is the new master browse server.

In the case of a tie between two browsers of equal ranking, the browser "wins" the election if it has been running longer than the sender. If, not the machine with the lowest alphabetical or numerical NetBIOS name wins. For example, a server named "A" wins over "B," and "1" wins over "2."

6.3.2
Heir Apparent: The Running Election State

The browser that wins the election next enters a state called *Running Election State*. The first task at hand is to broadcast a Request Election message. This message is sent after a predetermined delay, based on the browser's current role.[68] Up to four such Election Request messages are sent. If no reply is received, the browser that sent the requests is promoted to Master Browse Server. If it receives a reply that another machine won the election, however, and that machine is current Master Browse Server, then the browser demotes itself to Backup Browse Server.

6.4
Browse Request and Reply

When a user clicks access the *Network* GUI, net view command-line, or simply points the Run command to \\servername\[sharename], the *computer browser service* on that machine sends out a broadcast message called the *Get Backup List Request*. The master browse server then replies with a unicast message containing the list of up to three backup browse servers. The client chooses one of these machines and sends another message, requesting the content of the browse list. The selected browse server (if functioning properly) then replies with the requested information. The following diagram shows this process:

6.5
"I Do Not Know the LAN"

Removal of a NetBIOS name from the browse list can take considerably longer than the registration process. This is by design: to account for missed transmissions, the

---

[68]This information is detailed in the TechNet article on the Computer Browser Service: http://technet.microsoft.com/en-us/library/cc737661%28WS.10%29.aspx

master browser does not remove a node form its browse list until 3 broadcast cycles (36 minutes) have passed. When a machine is shutdown gracefully, it broadcasts a notification to the master browser that it will no longer be available. The master browse server removes the entry from its browse list, then propagates this change to the other browse masters on the network. Assuming these updates work as intended, the name of the machine being removed from the workgroup or domain is updated within the 3 broadcast cycles (36 minutes) mentioned above.

If a machine is not gracefully shutdown, however, this notification is never sent. It then remains in the browse list of the master browse server for up to 36 minutes, or until the 3rd broadcast cycle has come and gone without a reply from the disconnected server. The master browser then notifies the domain master browse server on its next update cycle. The master browse server then notifies remote master browse servers on other subnets, which in turn update their backup browse servers. Since each of these updates occur at 12-minute increments, the non-graceful removal of a machine from a large network may require up to 72 minutes for the browse list to fully propagate. This explains why a disruption in the normal communication between a browse master server and its clients can result in "phantom" machines that appear in the Network list (or net view), but are not reachable as resources. (At the network level, of course, the machine would not respond to ping.)

6.6
The King Is Dead! Long Live the King!

As noted above, a graceful shutdown of a client machine results in a notification to the master browser. If a master browser is gracefully shutdown, it forces an election and another machine assumes the role of new master. If the master browser is not gracefully shutdown—if a hardware failure or network disruption of some kind occurs—a delay may occur before browsing can be active again on the subnet. The first client to request the browse list and not receive a reply will force an election. Otherwise, a full broadcast cycle (12 minutes) might ensue before the backup master browse server determines that the master server is unresponsive, and forces an election. Within another 12 minutes (allowing for replication to occur), the new master browse server is operational, and browsing can resume.

CHAPTER 7:
ACTIVE DIRECTORY®

7.1
Active Directory Terms and Concepts[69]

Active Directory (AD) is the Microsoft implementation of the Lightweight Directory Access Protocol (LDAP), and is comprised of two basic roles. The first is a *directory* (also called *data store*) in which *objects* are stored. An object is a representation of a real thing, such as a person or business. Think of a directory like the phone book, where an object would be a listing for a person or business. Attached to this object are various attributes, such as name, address, or phone number. Extending this concept to resources that exist within a computer network, we see that Active Directory objects come in various forms:

1. Shared resources: printers, servers, databases
2. Credentials & security: User account, computer account, security or distribution groups
3. Other information: domains, applications, services, security policies

In other words, a vast array of information can be stored in Active Directory. An object for a user could be as simple as a login name and password, or as complex as the users phone number, email address, physical address, department, title, security groups,

---

[69] For a full explanation of Active Directory, see
http://technet.microsoft.com/en-us/library/cc782657%28WS.10%29.aspx. The information is specific to Windows 2003, but most of the concepts are universal across versions (Windows 2000 and above).

and so forth. Similarly, a network printer might be an object in Active Directory, with attributes that point not only to its IP address, but physical location, make and model, and other information used for easy reference. By centralizing all of this information into Active Directory, the directory becomes a one-stop-shop for data related to users and other resources on the network, accessible from applications that are able to query the directory.

The second role of Active Directory is as a *directory service*, or program, that interact with the directory itself and make this information accessible to users or applications. As such, the directory service is a server-side application that "listens" on the network for inbound queries from a client. In the case of Active Directory, the server-side application is called, collectively, Active Directory in Windows 2000 and Windows 2003/2003 R2, or Active Directory Domain Services in Windows 2008/2008 R2. Active Directory as a directory service is thus the *namespace* upon which the entire structure of a Windows domain exists. Recall that we first encountered the term *namespace* in Chapter 1, with reference to the Internet. At the top of the hierarchy was a series of Top-Level Domains (TLDs), such as *.com*, *.net*, and so forth. Active Directory both supplements and extends this basic namespace concept, being based upon the DNS structure used on the Internet. As such, both DNS and Active Directory must be functioning properly for a Windows domain to be usable. This is because though they are separate services, DNS as used on a Windows domain is *integrated* with Active Directory. (More will be said about this in a future section.)

7.2
"Seeing the Forest for the Trees"

In days of old, when men were bold and Novell was king of the Local Area Network, its NetWare operating system held the lion's share of the fileserver market. Originally designed as a server-centric system, all user accounts were stored in a database on each server. This meant that usage of multiple servers required multiple accounts, perhaps with different logins. Starting with NetWare version 4, however, things changed dramatically. Instead of being server-centric, user accounts and other network resource information was stored in an LDAP directory called Novell Directory Service (NDS), which could be replicated between servers. The name given to an NDS schema was *tree*. Given the fierce competition between Microsoft and Novell,[70] and the fact that both were beginning to

---

[70] Legend has it that a codename (or nickname) for the project that became known as Windows NT Server was "Visine." This was because the logo for Novell was red, and NT was intended to

base their products on standards designed for the Internet (such as LDAP and DNS), it was not surprising that the concepts and even terminology was similar between the two offerings. Whereas Novell called their schema a *tree*, Microsoft dubbed the top level of their Active Directory namespace a *forest*. Within a forest, one or more domains can be created, and within a domain, one or more *child domains* can be created. An upper-level domain is therefore called a *parent domain*. Finally, domains that share a common namespace (such as parent and child) form a structure called a *tree* within the Active Directory *forest*.[71]

In the example below, our XYZ Corporation has create an Active Directory topology with the forest name *xyz.local*. As the first domain created within this forest, *xyz.local* is also designated as the *root forest domain*. In order to separate its East and West divisions, distinct domains have been created for each within the *xyz.local* forest, named (conveniently enough), *west.xyz.local* and *east.xyz.local*. This has another added benefit: no two objects within an Active Directory domain can have the same name. By having separate domains, the divisions of XYZ Corporation can name the objects in their respective directories the same, if they wish. Thus, there can be a *sales.west.xyz.local* and a *sales.east.xyz.local*. The *sales* child domain would thus be part of its respective tree. Finally, XYZ has decided separate its C-

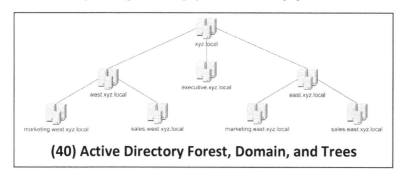

(40) Active Directory Forest, Domain, and Trees

"get the red out." A bit of research on Google has not been able to confirm this, but the story is amusing nonetheless. ☺

[71] Not surprisingly, the confusion these turns-of-phrase elicited was considerable. The situation was exacerbated by the fact that many organizations already invested in Novell licensing began switching to all-Windows network topologies due to the need for both file-serving and application servers. Thus, admins had to learn two sets of terminology that looked interchangeable, but were not.

Given the wide adoption of Windows for the desktop in an era when client/server technology was on the ascendency, it was understandable that many more developers began to write their applications to run on a Windows NT platform than for Novell NetWare. The fact that NT and its successors had a GUI interface at the server console while Novell's remained heavily focused on command-line (CLI), at least until later iterations may also have played a role. Rightly or wrongly, the GUI made Windows appear easier to manage than CLI-centric NetWare or UNIX. In an ironic twist, Novell some time ago abandoned true NetWare and is now heavily invested in UNIX and Linux platforms, with which it has integrated products like NDS and GroupWise email server that used to run on NetWare.

level executives into their own domain, called *executive.xyz.local*. Note that this is not a child or parent of either the East or West divisions, but a totally separate domain within the *xyz.local* forest.

7.2.1
Trust, But Verify

A *trust relationship* allows resources in one domain to be available to users in another domain. By default, a *transitive* and *bidirectional* trust relationship is created between a parent and child domain or a domain and its root. *Transitive* means that the trust can extend beyond the immediate object of the trust to others above it. For example, a transitive trust allows child domain *sales.west.xyz.local* to not only have a trust relationship with its parent, *west.xyz.local*, but also with the parent of its parent—in this case, the root forest domain *xyz.local*. A non-transitive trust would conversely allow the child to trust the parent, but would not extend beyond that to the higher level and thus all the way to the root of the forest. *Bidirectional* means that the child trusts the parent, and *vice versa*. When combined, a *transitive bidirectional* or *transitive 2-way* trust means that every domain within the forest has an automatic trust relationship with every other domain. Thus, a user in the *executive.xyz.local* domain could, given that proper permissions are assigned, access resources in one of the other domains, or in the root forest domain itself.

The power of trust relationships for end-users is that access is allowed seamlessly across boundaries such as domains or even forests. The power of trust relationships from a system administration perspective is the ability to simplify the task of assigning permissions to resources throughout the forest. Note that the trust itself does not allow a particular user access to a particular resource. That access is still controlled by the *Access Control List* for that object as stored in Active Directory. What the trust does, however, is allow the *possibility* of a user in one domain to access a resource in another.

7.2.2
One Domain Or Many?

The question of how many domains should be created and how they should be organized is an important question, and one that should not be answered lightly when designing and implementing Active Directory. For small organizations, the *root forest domain* may be the only one ever created. As such, it is here that all objects will reside. All domain controllers on the network (including global catalog servers) will be members of this root forest domain. In such a topology, the distinction between forest and domain is blurred: the forest *is* the domain.

In larger organizations, things can remain simple (one domain spanning one or more physical locations, IP subnets, and Active Directory sites) or get very complicated. The complexity of a topology such as is described above for XYZ Corporation takes things somewhat to their logical extreme, and may well have been put in place for political or organizational rather than technical reasons. For example, suppose that each business unit (East and West) maintains their own IT staff. These persons could be designated as Active Directory *Domain Administrators* of their respective domains, and have full access to the resources therein, but not to the root forest domain or the *executive.xyz.local* domain. Furthermore, suppose that the sales group wants to retain control over their own resources, and be able to add or delete users from their Active Directory child domain without calling upon the technical staff that oversees the *west.xyz.local* or *east.xyz.local* domains. In the interests of "local control," separate domains (and child domains) have been created, and permissions assigned to various individuals to have administrative access to certain portions of Active Directory. Granting such access is known as *delegation*, for it allows a lower-privilege user to control certain aspects of the directory, but not the whole.

7.3
The Object of Our Attention

7.3.1
"GUID"—Rhymes With "Squid"

We said above that an *object* is a representation of a real entity (person or thing), to which various attributes are attached that describe that entity. When an Active Directory object is created, some attributes are created by default, while others are entered manually. For example, a user object includes input for first and/or last name, login name, and password. To these attributes, Active Directory adds a 128-bit piece of data called the *Globally Unique Identifier* (GUID), often pronounced "gwid." The GUID is a unique pointer to the object that is this user account. Think of a GUID like a person's Social Security Number (SSN). Most people will not spend their entire lives at the same address. Likewise, a person's name (such as a woman who marries and adopts her husband's surname) may change over time. But despite having lived in multiple homes with multiple physical addresses or having had multiple phone numbers over the years, one thing that never changes (usually) is the 8-digit Social Security Number assigned to that person by the Social Security Administration of the United States. Like the GUID, this SSN uniquely identifies the person in question, and thus is a required form of identification for obtaining a driver's license, filling out a job application, filing one's taxes, and so forth.

Within an Active Directory forest, no two objects can have the same GUID. An object that is deleted and subsequently recreated—even if assigned the attributes such as username and password—will not bear the original GUID, but be assigned a new one, for it is seen as a new, unique object within the directory. Thus, all properties and attributes associated with the original object must be applied to the recreated object if this is to replace the deleted object. To reiterate, the GUID assigned to an object within Active Directory **never** changes. Changes to attributes (such as changing the user information or login name) does not change the GUID. In organizations that create multiple domains within their Active Directory forest, the GUID is the unique identifier across all domains within that forest. As such, while moving an object from one domain to another affects other attributes (detailed below), the GUID remains untouched.

7.3.2
"Schema For Me, Long Beach!"

The *schema* is a description of the *object classes*, or types of objects, present within the directory. Each object class is then assigned a list of attributes that it has or may have, and the object class that may be its "parent." This schema information is then stored as objects within Active Directory; this design allows Active Directory to managed all information related to objects (or information about objects) together. Applications that interact with Active Directory use the schema to determine what attributes an object *must* have or *might* have, as well as the syntax and data structure of those objects. Certain applications also require and apply changes to the schema, adding additional attributes or object classes for use with the functionality of the program being installed. An example of this is Microsoft Exchange, which makes a change to the Active Directory schema when being installed. Schema changes can be nerve-wracking, since modifying the Active Directory structure brings the risk of bringing the network down. After all, a failed schema change could render Active Directory unusable.[72]

---

[72]Like all data on the network, Active Directory should be backed-up regularly. The NTBackup utility, included with Windows Server, as well as 3rd-party software such as Backup Exec, can backup and restore the System State, which includes the Active Directory databases.

7.3.3
The Security Principal Name (SPN)

Objects created within the Active Directory schema follow one of several naming conventions. The first is called the Security Principal Name (SPN). An SPN is automatically assigned to three types of objects: user account, computer account, or group. Though it is common to think of authentication as related to users (a person "logs in" to the network and then begins to work), it is important that Active Directory actually maintains objects about computers and other resources as well. Computers accounts are assigned to Windows machines that are "joined" to the domain; thereafter, the computer account is used for authentication and access control purposes. Likewise, a group can be comprised of user accounts or computer accounts, and assigned permissions to grant or deny access to network resources. Each of these—the user object, computer object, or group object—is assigned an SPN unique to the domain in which it is created. When the object seeks to access resources to which it has been granted permissions, it must first authenticate against a domain controller for that domain. Finally, unlike the GUID discussed above, an SPN is not unique across domains, but must be unique within its own.

7.3.4
"Here's Looking At You, SID"

A Security Identifier (SID) is a number created by the security subsystem of Active Directory and assigned to an SPN—that is, to objects related to users, computers, or groups. The SID is assigned when the object is created, and it is to the SID that various operating system processes refer, rather than to the username or group name that is an attribute of the object. Like the GUID, deletion and recreation of a security-related object such as user, computer, or group, results in a new object with a unique SID assignment. Active Directory objects are protected by Access Control Entries (ACEs) that identify which users or groups are permitted to access a given resource. However, the ACE contains not usernames or group names, but SIDs; thus, if a user account is deleted and then recreated, even if the attributes are identical to the original object, the ACE will not recognize the new object as having rights to the resource in question, nor associate it in any way with the old object so as to permit transfer of permissions. In other words, the machine will do precisely what it has been instructed to do: compare the SID of the object requesting access to the list of SIDs authorized to gain access, and allow or deny that access on the basis of this information alone.

7.3.4.1
A Ghost of a Chance

An understanding of what a SID is and does is critical within two arena: disk imaging and virtualization. Actually, both can be considered at once, because the underlying concepts are the same. The long-popular Ghost software (and its competitors) allow for an *image* of a physical computer to be made and then applied to other machines. The image is a sector-by-sector copy of the hard drive(s), done at the bit level. This is then written to the target system to produce a duplicate of the original machine, including (unless changed) the hostname, NetBIOS name, IP address (if static) and...wait for it...the System Identifier.

Because no two systems can share a SID, this immediately begs the question: how shall the new computer be assigned a new SID? The answer is a utility called *sysprep*, available as a free download from Microsoft, but also included in the disk imaging software and incorporated into its own functionality. When executed, the sysprep utility creates and assigned a new Security Identifier for the computer on which it is run. As a result, at least from a SID perspective, the machine is again "unique" on the network. Depending on the tool used (sysprep alone vs. 3rd party imaging software) it may be necessary to script or otherwise account for a change in the NetBIOS name and/or hostname of the computer. Also, if the source machine used to create the image was assigned a static IP address, this will need to be changed as well.

A similar idea lies behind virtualization, such as VMWare. ESX, in its ability to create a *virtual machine* (VM) with the desired configuration and then convert that VM into a *template* from which other VMs can be created. As part of this functionality, ESX provides a mechanism for "customizing" the resulting virtual machine, including a means by which a random computer name (NetBIOS and DNS hostname) and SID can be created.

7.3.5
Of Names, Common and Distinguished

As mentioned above, Active Directory is a directory service compliant with the Lightweight Directory Access Protocol (LDAP). As a result, access to objects within Active Directory is done through LDAP queries. Familiarity with certain terms related to LDAP is therefore helpful when working with Active Directory. The first of these is the Common Name (CN), which is used with the *user* object class. This is the name of the object itself. The Organization Unit (OU) is a virtual folder in which objects are stored in the directory. For example, the Sales team might have an OU called Sales, in which all members of that department are included.

An OU is different from a group, in that a group is associated with security (access to resources), while an OU is a means of grouping objects within the directory structure.[73] The *Domain Component* (DC) refers to the domain name. Finally, the *Distinguished Name* (DN) is the complete listing of an object with respect to the root of the directory. This is comparable to the Fully Qualified Domain Name (FQDN) used with DNS. For example, the computer used by a user named Joe in the Sales department of the West division of XYZ Corporation might have the FQDN *joelaptop.sales.west.xyz.local*.

In Active Directory, the user account object for Joe would have the following Distinguished Name (DN):

cn=Joe,ou=Sales,dc=west,dc=xyz,dc=local[74]

7.3.6
The User Principal Name (UPN)

Among the attributes assigned to a user account in Active Directory is the *User Principal Name* (UPN). The UPN is written in the format user@domainname, and is independent of the user's object Distinguished Name (DN). As such, even if the user object is moved or renamed, the UPN remains unchanged. The advantage of using a UPN is that the domain is not required to be entered separately, as it is included in the username. Another method of doing the same function is to enter the username as *DOMAIN\username*.

---

[73] While an OU is thus (primarily) an administrative method for breaking up a large directory into smaller, more manageable pieces, Active Directory adds a unique function as well. Group Policy Objects (GPOs), a method of applying security to users or computers/applications, can be set at the OU level. Thus, the Sales OU might have a GPO that configures specific things about their user accounts or computers and applications. These policies are set by the administrator, and work behind-the-scenes, usually seamlessly to the end users.

[74] Such LDAP-intensive work comes into play with 3rd-party applications that interact with Active Directory as a generic LDAP directory. For example, an program might be written to retrieve information from Active Directory using LDAP query language, rather than through the Application Programming Interface (API) structure provided by Microsoft. Such an application might have originally been written for another platform, such as UNIX or Linux, and is thus not designed to understand the subtleties of Microsoft's implantation of the LDAP standards. The reason for including this level of detail here is that Active Directory *is* an LDAP directory, and so those who delve deep enough into Windows networking are bound to encounter the terminology and syntax associated with LDAP at some point. ☺

7.4
Active Directory Sites

An Active Directory *site* is a grouping of computers in one or more IP subnets, generally at the same physical location and connected via a Local Area Network (LAN). For example, the West division of our fictional company, XYZ Corporation, might be located in a particular office building or city, and would thus be represented in Active Directory as a site. Sites are connected together by Wide Area Network (WAN) links, which are usually much slower than the LAN speeds used within each site. In order to serve users more effectively, it is common practice to locate one or more domain controllers (DCs) at each site. These DCs then replicate all or portions of the Active Directory forest between themselves, thus keeping all users updated with the latest changes to the directory structure.

7.4.1
Sites and Replication

Active Directory is designed to function with sites in mind—that is, when 2 or more Active Directory sites are configured, the system assumes that these are not local to each other, and therefore are connected with limited bandwidth. As a result, Active Directory is designed to minimize replication traffic between sites, thus leaving bandwidth available for other purposes. It is also possible to schedule replication to occur at a given timeframe, to avoid bottlenecks that might occur. For example, it might be that Active Directory replication is needed only one daily, and that the limited WAN links between 2 sites is needed for other applications as well. The Active Directory replication could then be scheduled to occur after-hours, so as to avoid conflicts with other applications that require the WAN link during business hours.

What this means, however, is that the balance between maintaining replication of Active Directory information across sites (so one site is not using stale records) must be balanced with performance and user experience. The more WAN bandwidth is available for Active Directory replication, the more often this replication can occur, and the less likely that stale records will be encountered. For example, suppose that a user at Site A changes his/her password. The change is made on a domain controller at that location, and will be immediately seen by other users or applications that authenticate against that DC. The change should also be replicated relatively quickly to other DCs within the same site, since they are connected by LAN links that should provide more-than-adequate bandwidth for the task. However, depending on the WAN configuration to other sites, and the schedule set for site-to-site replication, the change may not be reflected on a domain controller at Site B for some time. Thus, were the same user to login to a machine that authenticates against a DC at that other site, he/she might find that the old password is still expected. Because the Active Directory replication has not completed yet, the other DC does not yet know that a change has been made to the directory.

7.4.2
Sites vs. Domains

Finally, the following must be taken into account with respect to Active Directory sites. First, *sites* and *domains* are independent entities—that is, there is no necessary connection or correlation between the two. While sites are related to the *physical* topology of the network (segments and subnets), domains represent the logical structure of the organization and its namespace. A single site might contain multiple domains. For example, the Sales department at the West division of XYZ Corporation might have its own child domain (sales.west.xyz.local). If the Accounting department also has its own child domain (marketing.west.xyz.local), both child domains would be logical extensions of the west.xyz.local domain, but the machines and users that are members of the 2 domains would be located in the same Active Directory Site. Conversely, a sales organization might have a single domain with users spread across multiple geographic locations, such as branch offices in different cities. These users would be members of the same Active Directory domain, but could be authenticating against domain controllers that are physically located in separate places and are grouped into appropriate sites. The Active Directory replication done between sites would thus be replicating a single domain across multiple sites.

Sites are configured using the Active Directory Sites and Services MMC. It is here that various divisions based on subnet or network segment are added to the directory, so that Active Directory replication between DCs can be planned and managed according to the bandwidth available.

7.5
Active Directory Organization

Active Directory is organized by several means. The first is at the forest level. One or more domains may be created within the forest, and will be displayed accordingly in the Active Directory management tool (to be detailed below). Within a domain, the primary means of organizing or categorizing objects is through the use of *Organization Units* (OUs). An OU is like a folder in a file system. Objects can be placed in an OU, and OUs can be placed within other OUs. This process is called *nesting*.

Recall from Chapter 1 that Ethernet protocols are encapsulated within one another—that is, an application-layer protocol like SMB is encapsulated into an IP packet, which is then encapsulated into an Ethernet frame. At each stage of this process, the higher-level data unit is effectively hidden from view, for the lower-level cannot read its contents. Instead, it reads the header information attached to the data unit, and thus determines how it is to be processed. Encapsulation thus refers to the lowest-level data unit, within which other data units are contained. Parsing this structure involves removing each layer, one by one, like an onion.

The concept of nesting is different, and is related to the DNS name space. An OU within another OU does not lose its identity, but is instead referenced in relation to the root of the directory. Like DNS, this can makes for a long string called a *Distinguished Name* (DN). In this case, these are separated by commas rather than dots. The more levels of OUs involved, the longer the DN string.

7.6
Under the Hood:
The Mechanics of a Domain Controller

The act of "creating" an Active Directory domain itself is accomplished with the **dcpromo** command on a machine running a compatible version of the Windows Server operating system and having the prerequisite services, such as DNS, available on the network. While DNS can be anywhere, and can actually be a non-Microsoft version of the DNS services, it is common to install the Microsoft DNS service onto the machine that will become the domain controller. [75] The **dcpromo** process establishes the name of the forest and/or domain. Recall that if a single domain is created, it is known as the *forest root domain*. The server is thereafter said to have been *promoted* to DC. Assuming DNS is running locally, the server now hosts two separate and distinct namespace directories: one for Active Directory, the other for DNS. When utilizing Active Directory-integrated DNS, however, the DNS information is actually stored within the Active Directory

---

[75] Windows 2000 and 2003 installed DNS separately from Active Directory, such that DNS must be installed from the CD or installation media prior to running **dcpromo**. Thankfully, Microsoft has changed this such that DNS is automatically installed when the **dcpromo** process is started.

database. In this way, it can be replicated to other domain controllers within the same domain. Active Directory domains (i.e., Windows 2000 and above) are capable of replicating their data to one or more additional DCs, which act as peers. Running **dcpromo** on subsequent servers adds them as additional domain controllers to the same domain, or creates additional domains or subdomains, as specified during the process.

7.6.1
AD *à la* mode

Mixed mode refers to a situation where domain controllers running different versions of Windows Server co-exist on a network. For example, suppose that a domain was originally created on Windows 2003. Now suppose that for various reasons, the decision has been made to upgrade the domain to Windows 2008 R2. When a server running the newer OS version is added to the network and **dcpromo** is executed on it, it will become either the first DC of a new forest or domain, or the second DC of the existing domain. If the intention is to upgrade the domain from Windows 2003 to Windows 2008 R2, the latter choice must be made. The result, when finished, is a Windows 2008 R2 domain running in *mixed mode*. Certain functionality accessible only with a Windows 2008 R2 domain will not be available, so as to remain backward compatible with the Windows 2003 DCs.

Native mode refers to a change made to this domain after all DCs running anything other than Windows 2008 R2 have been demoted and/or upgraded. Only when all DCs are running the same (most recent) version of Windows Server can the domain be configured for *native mode*. This process enables functionality that was not available in *mixed mode*, and means that no DCs can be added to the network that are not running the same version of Windows as the existing DCs. Servers running operating systems other than Windows 2008 R2 can still be *members* of the domain, but cannot serve as domain controllers.

7.6.2
Active Directory Naming Contexts

Information stored on the DC is categorized as *domain*, *schema*, or *configuration* data. These segments are also called *partitions*, and are the units replicated to other domain controllers for the same domain on the network. The *domain partition* contains all of the objects for a given domain. This information is then replicated to other domain controllers for that same domain. The *schema partition* holds all object types that can be created within Active Directory. Since this information is common to all domains, the schema partition is replicated to all DCs in the forest. Finally, the *configuration partition* holds replication topology and metadata. Applications that are "aware" of Active Directory store information common to all domains in a given domain tree or forest in the configuration partition, which like the schema partition, is then replicated to all domain controllers in the forest.

7.6.3
The Global Catalog

A fourth partition type exists only on a domain controller that has been configured as a *global catalog* (GC). A global catalog plays two roles within the Active Directory structure: *logon* and *querying*. In short, it is the GC that allows a user to login to a client machine with domain privileges. (The GC also provides authentication for the machine that is a member of the domain, since the computer itself has an account, just as the user does.) Querying comes into play in larger organizations where multiple domains exist. In such an environment, the GC allows for a search across domains. For example, a user at the West division XYZ Corporate (a child domain of xyz.local) wishes to send an email to a user in the East division (another child domain of xyz.local). Without the global catalog, the user in east.xyz.local would have no way of querying for information contained in the other domain, since east and west are both child domains of the same parent (xyz.local), and have no direct connection between them. A non-GC domain controller in either domain is unaware of user accounts in the other, but a GC *is* aware, because this information is replicated forest-wide.

This forest-wide querying and login capability is made possible by the fourth type of partition, stored only on a GC. That partition is a *partial* (read-only) or *full* (read/write) replica of the domain directory partition for all domains in the forest. In other words, while a "regular" domain controller holds a replicated copy of all objects for its own domain(s), a global catalog domain controller hold a replicated copy of all objects for all domains. This is accomplished as follows: first, a non-GC domain controller replicates itself with a GC. The GC now holds a copy of all objects for the "foreign" domain. This GC, in turn, replicates its information with another GC, which may have replicated with another non-GC for another domain. When these various strata of replication have completed, the GCs hold all objects for all domains, while the domain controllers related to the individual domains themselves hold only objects for their respective domain or child domain.

7.6.4
"FSMO"—Rhymes With "Gizmo"

The Naming Contexts outlined above are created when the Active Directory root forest domain is created—that is, when the first Windows Server is promoted to DC for the forest. This first DC also assumes two specific responsibilities. First, it becomes the first global catalog for the forest. Secondly, it is assigned a collection of roles called the *Operations Master* or *Flexible Single Master Operation* (FSMO), pronounced *fizmo*. In the event that additional DCs are added later, FSMO roles (in whole or in part) can be assigned to other DCs using the Active Directory snap-ins for the Microsoft Management Console (MMC) or at the command-line with the *Ntdsutil.exe* utility. There are five FSMO roles in all. The first two roles are forest-wide and thus assigned to one domain controller in the root forest domain. The remaining three are domain-wide and assigned to one domain controller per domain.

The *Schema Master* role is the first of the forest-wide roles, and is responsible for management of the Active Directory schema. This role is also required when an *extension* is to be made to the schema. An extension adds objects and/or attributes to Active Directory. Certain applications, such as Microsoft Exchange, require a schema extension. The schema is also changed when the first server running a newer Windows Server version is promoted to become a domain controller in an existing domain.

The second forest-wide role is that of *Domain Naming Master*. This role is required when domains are to be created or removed. It is also required in order to install or uninstall *application partitions* from the forest. An *application partition* is a specialized configuration within Active Directory that allows a particular application to use a designated name space (similar to a domain). This data can also be replicated only to designated domain controllers, as may be required.

The *Relative ID (RID) Master* is first of the three domain-wide roles and assigned to only one domain controller per domain. When a domain controller creates a security principal object—user account, computer account, or security group—it attaches a security identifier (SID) to the object. This SID consists of a domain SID (a common name that identifies the domain in which it was created) and a relative identifier (RID) that is unique to each security principal SID created within the domain. Each DC in a domain is allocated a group of RIDs (called a *RID pool*) that are then assigned to the security principal objects that domain controller creates. This pool is managed by the domain controller that holds the *RID Master*.

The second domain-wide role is the *PDC emulator*. One original purpose of the PDC emulator was to "emulate" the Primary Domain Controller functionality of a Windows NT domain. This allowed computers running Windows NT (including servers) to participate in a Windows 2000 network during the transition or upgrade period. On a network running only Windows 2000 or above, however, this role is irrelevant. Nonetheless, the PDC emulator performs other tasks on a Windows 2000/2003 domain. The first relates to password changes: any change of a user's password performed on another domain controller is preferentially replicated to the PDC emulator as well. Likewise, authentication failures are forwarded to the PDC emulator before a "bad password" message is relayed to the user, and account lockouts due to multiple logon failures are processed by the PDC emulator. Finally, creation or modification of a Group Policy Object (GPO) is performed against the copy hosed on the PDU emulator's SYSVOL share, unless otherwise configured.

The *Infrastructure Master* is the third domain-wide role, and is applicable to the referential relationship between objects in different domains. In short, the domain controller holding the *Infrastructure Master* role is responsible for maintaining this information.

7.6.5
Oh, No! Oh, No! The FSMO Doesn't Go!

The first domain controller for a forest or domain retains all FSMO roles unless these have been reconfigured via the MMC or command-line. But what if additional domain controllers are added later, and this original machine is subsequently shutdown or (worse yet) reformatted and re-tasked? The answer is simple: Active Directory will continue to function fine until such time as a change that requires FSMO authentication is attempted. Such a time would be an extension of the schema (perhaps to install a new Active Directory-aware application, like Exchange). If the FSMO roles are not available, the process will fail. How then can this be resolved, if the machine that hosted those roles is no longer available?

Just such a scenario calls for a special procedure, run from the command-line, which *seizes* the FSMO roles and assigns them to a DC of the administrators choice. Note that this is a last-resort process. If the machine that originally held the FSMO roles should be turned back on *after* manual/forced seizure of those roles by another domain controller, the results would be unpredictable at best. FSMO roles can only be held by one machine at a time.

7.7
Active Directory Replication

Active Directory is a *multimaster* system whereby information from one domain controller (DC) can be replicated to others, if available. As peer systems, each DC holds a read-and-write copy of the directory.[76] Replication occurs both within Active Directory sites (*intra-site* replication) and between sites (*inter-site* replication). Thus, any changes made to the directory on one DC is propagated automatically to other DCs within the same domain, as well as to the global catalog servers that service the Active Directory forest.

7.7.1
Active Directory Propagation

All the way back in Chapter 3, we discussed the importance of maintaining an accurate source of time that is common to all machines on the network, and the use of the Network Time Protocol to accomplish this feat. With respect to log files and other data that relies on a simple time-stamp, this is about more than being stickler for punctuality: having an accurate and common time source for all nodes (especially servers or appliances that generate logs) helps to ensure that timestamp on Server A is reasonably close to that used on Appliance B.

7.7.1.1
Update Sequence Numbers

When designing Active Directory, however, Microsoft wisely chose not to use timestamps as the means by which Active Directory records were compared and/or updated. Instead, Active Directory uses an Update Sequence Number (USN), a 64-bit value maintained by each domain controller. The USN is advanced with each update to the record. This information is then stored on the local DC. In addition to these local USN records, each DC also maintains a table of USNs received from replication partners. The highest USN received is stored in this table, and is updated as needed to replicate with other DCs. This means that replication is not *primarily* tied to or reliant upon having timestamps that are accurately synchronized across systems. It also means that should replication fail and be restarted, a simple comparison of the USNs between servers

---

[76] The exception is the *read-only domain controller* (RODC), a role available only in Windows 2008 and 2008 R2 systems running in native mode.

determines which has the authoritative record that is to be propagated to the peers.

7.7.1.2
The Property Version Number

In addition to the *Update Sequence Number*, Active Directory assigns to an object another property called the *Property Version Number* (PVN). Unlike a USN, which is managed on each domain controller independently, the PVN is applicable across all domain controllers. The PVN is initialized when a property is first written to an object. For example, when a user account is created, the initial password is assigned to the account and the PVN is initialized for that property. If the password is changed thereafter, the domain controller holding the record issues an *originating write* that increments the PVN.

A originating write is always and only performed on the DC initiating the change. For example, supposed that our user, whose workstation is communicating with DC1, changes his or her password. DC1 becomes the *originating* domain controller from which the *originating write* is initiated, thus incrementing the Property Version Number for the password property of the user account object. When DC1 subsequently propagates this change to other DCs, these are labeled *replication writes*, and do not increment the PVN. As a result, only the DC against which the change was initiated is able to change or advance the PVN, thus maintaining the integrity of the propagation of these changes to other domain controllers.

When a replicated change is received by a DC, the PVN of the data being replicated is compared to the local data. If the PVN of the change is higher than the local copy, the change is applied as an update. If the PVN is older than the local copy, it is presumed to be *stale* (outdated), and is discarded.

7.7.1.3
Replication Collisions

Because Active Directory is a *multi-master system*, changes to the property of an object can be made simultaneously on different domain controllers. The situation that can ensue is called a *replication collision*. A collision occurs when 2 criteria are met:

- A change to the property of the same object has been made on multiple DCs. As a result, the Update Sequence Number (USN) has been incremented on each domain controller against which the change was initiated

- The updates as applied to the property of the object has resulted in the Property Version Number (PVN) being incremented as well by multiple DCs, each of which issued an *originating write*.

Since these changes were made simultaneously, the USN is not helpful for determining which domain controller should be considered authoritative. In fact, both domain controllers in this instance would be considered authoritative, for each updated their USN as the result of a change made on the copy of Active Directory hosted on that server.

Unfortunately, the PVN may also been incremented. As a result, some other method must be in place to reconcile this situation and determine which update is to be applied and which are to be discarded.

It is here that the timestamp of the record comes into play. Given what has been outlined above, the normal method of determining which record is more up-to-date is not valid. In this situation (and this one *only*), Active Directory looks at the timestamps of the records. The one that is latest (i.e., most recent) is used to update the others. Note that Other than in this instance, the timestamp is never used to update Active Directory records.

7.8
Active Directory and DNS:
A Marriage Made In Redmond

In order to function properly, a Windows domain requires that compatible DNS services be configured on the network. (Microsoft's preference, of course, is that this DNS service be their own, running on a Windows Server.)[77] Nodes on the Windows network about to be created will be identified by their Fully Qualified Domain Name (FQDN). When Active Directory-integrated DNS services are used, hostnames added to the domain are also added to DNS.

---

[77] While it is possible to run a non-Microsoft DNS server with a Windows domain, this is not best practice. DNS, DHCP, and other network services can easily run alongside Active Directory on even a small server.

7.8.1
DNS In Depth

Active Directory follows the Domain Name Space convention. As a result, the name assigned to a Windows domain is identical in Active Directory and DNS. In the Domain Name Space hierarchy, the upper-most level, or *root*, is represented by a single dot (.). Fully-Qualified Domain names are written as strings of names separated by dots, with a trailing dot representing the root. For example, take the domain name for XYZ Corporation:

- *xyz.com. is* a domain under Top-Level Domain (TLD) *.com*
- *west.xyz.com* is a subdomain for the western division of the organization (logically and/or geographically defined)
- *mail.xyz.com* is a hostname for the email server

What distinguishes *mail.xyz.com* as hostname for an email server from *west.xyz.com* as a subdomain for a division of the company is not the naming convention itself, but the type of *record* used to store this information in DNS. A *record* is a piece of information that describes an entity, such as a server or domain, and includes information like the name, IP address, and (as applicable) other relevant data. Several types of records can be used to describe a domain:

An *A (Address) Record* is used to resolve a hostname to an IP Address. The A Record states that the given hostname can be located at the given IP.

A *CNAME (Canonical Name) Record* is used to create an alias for an existing hostname. This is distinct from the *A Record* in that it is merely a pointer. CNAME records are helpful to provide a means by which xyz.com and www.xyz.com point to the same IP address. This allows the URL to be entered into a browser with or without the "www" prepended, and still resolve correctly.

An *MX (Mail Exchanger) Record* is a service record that specifies where (i.e., to what hostname) email for the domain is to be delivered. MX records include a *priority* assignment (a numerical value) that allows multiple mail servers to be configured for redundancy. A lower number indicates precedence; the host whose MX record has the lowest priority number becomes the default location to which all mail is routed. In the event of identical MX record priority assignments, incoming mail will be delivered to both hosts, though the means by which this is accomplished (Round Robin, mail server load, or some other priority scheme) is dependent on factors outside of DNS itself.[78]

---

[78] A company may have hardware load balancers in place, for example, which would augment or decide this based on rules set there.

An *NS (Name Server) Record* indicates the hostname(s) of Authoritative Name Servers for the domain. The Primary Name Server for a domain is the "master" server against which other DNS servers compare their records, and from which they receive updates. Secondary and tertiary servers may also be listed. Finally, other servers not listed in the NS records may have cached copies of information about the domain, retrieved as part of previous queries. (Recall that when a DNS performs a recursive lookup—i.e., points outside itself to answer a query not resolvable by its own records—it caches the answer that is received so as to avoid having to perform the same lookup again, within a given period of time—as determined by the TTL settings of the records retrieved).

A *PTR (Pointer) Record* is used in *Reverse DNS* (RDNS) lookups. Rather than finding the IP for a given hostname, an RDNS query seeks the hostname associated with a known IP.

An SOA (Start of Authority) Record contains the following:

- The *Primary Authoritative Name Server* indicates the DNS server to be queried first for information about the domain.
- Contact information about the domain, such as the name and email address of the registered party—that is, an individual, or representative of the organization in whose name the domain is registered.
- The SOA *Serial Number* increments each time a change is made to the records for that domain. Secondary and tertiary name servers compare the serial number in their SOA record for a given domain to the serial number of the SOA on the primary name server, and thus know when to update their own records.
- The *Refresh* value (in seconds) indicates the length of time a secondary or tertiary name server should wait to contact the primary name server and *refresh*, or update, its records. The smaller this number, the more often the name servers will update their records; thus, a short Refresh time means that changes to records related to the domain can be propagated more quickly between name servers.
- A *Retry* value (in seconds) indicates the time a secondary or tertiary name server should wait before trying to connect and compare/refresh its records, in the event that the previous connection was refused by the primary server.
- The *Expire* value (in seconds) indicates how long a secondary or tertiary name server should hold its cached copy of DNS information for this domain, in the event that retries fail, before considering it expired or "stale."
- Finally, the *Minimum* value (in seconds) indicates how long name servers not listed in the NS records should hold information about this domain in cache.

An *SRV (Server) Record* is like an A Record in that it maps a hostname to an IP address. Unlike an A Record, however, a SRV record includes other information about the services running on that host. SRV records take the form *_Service._Protocol.DnsDomainName*, where *Service* is the name of a service (background program) running on the host, *Protocol* is the IP protocol used by that service (TCP or UDP) and *DnsDomainName* is the name of the domain of which the host is a member.[79]

7.8.2
Windows DNS Management

Active Directory-integrated DNS is managed using the *DNS Manager* MMC. The screenshot below shows the *_kerberos* and *_ldap* records that point to various domain controllers for the *hisc.local* domain. Note that each section of the FQDN (separated by dots) is displayed as a folder or subfolder within the MMC.

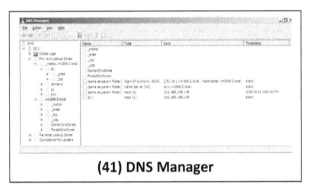

(41) DNS Manager

7.8.3
Domain Login and the SRV Record

When a domain controller starts up, the *Netlogon* service registers an SRV record with DNS. The records are stored in the form *_ldap._tcp.dc._msdcs.DnsDomainName*, where the *DnsDomainName* portion is the name of the Active Directory domain. For example, the root forest domain *xyz.local* would have an SRV record of *_ldap._tcp.dc.msdcs.xyz.local*. This SRV record is used to map the directory services provided by Active Directory to the DNS computer name of the domain controller.

When a client machine logs into the domain, it queries DNS for this SRV record in order to find a domain controller. If it is unable to find the DNS server, or if the SRV record and its related records are not present in DNS, the workstation cannot find Active Directory. This can result in a long wait while the system attempts to find the records it needs. If this process (which can take 15 minutes or so to complete) fails, the system will resort to NetBIOS broadcast to find the domain controller. It is then able to authenticate against the network. The root cause of this issue is that DNS is misconfigured on the workstation or server, or not working at all.[80]

---

[79] For a full discussion of SRV Resource Records and their use in Active Directory domain environments, see http://technet.microsoft.com/en-us/library/cc961719.aspx.

[80] For a more thorough explanation of the logon process for Windows XP on a domain, see http://support.microsoft.com/kb/314861.

7.8.4
Caveat Admin (Let the technician beware!)

A new installation of Active Directory presents the admin with a great deal of latitude as to its design and configuration. With freedom comes responsibility, however, and so (at least) two very important things must be borne in mind when planning an Active Directory environment. The first is straightforward, insofar as it cannot be overcome: Active Directory can only be installed on a certain versions of Windows Server. Windows Server Web Edition, introduced with the release of Windows Server 2003 cannot be used to host Active Directory.[81] Standard and above support multiple domain controllers and multiple domains or subdomains, and are scalable to very large proportions. Owing to its name, conversely, Small Business Server (SBS) or Small Business Edition (SBE) is a separate product that supports only one domain controller at the root of the domain, though additional member servers can be added; these cannot be another SBS/SBE machine, but must be running the "full" version Windows Server. This means, for example, that a network running Small Business Server cannot have another server also running SBS installed and joined to the same domain.[82] In other words, in the case where server hardware must be upgraded or replaced, it will be necessary to create a new domain on the new server and then transfer or create the user and other accounts between the two domains.

The second warning is more involved, and relates to how *not* to name an Active Directory domain. It *is* possible to choose whatever name is desired. One could, for example, choose to name the domain *mynetwork.com*. The domain controller for this domain might then become *server.mynetwork.com*. Client machines added thereafter might be *pc1.mynetwork.com*, and so forth. DNS will be populated with this information, and all will be well…or will it?

One day, a user will come to you and ask why, though he/she can browse anywhere else on the Internet, it is not possible to reach the website with URL http://www.mynetwork.com. After scratching your head and doing the obligatory Google searches, it might (finally) dawn on you that the root cause of your frustration is seated in your chair. ☺ The reason for this is that you named your Windows domain *mynetwork.com* without considering the implications. In short, someone "out there" has registered this domain name to be used on the public Internet, and is very well hosting a website, the

---

[81] As the name suggests, Web Server Edition is designed for use a web hosting platform. While it can be joined to a domain as a member, it cannot host applications or network services such as Active Directory, DNS, DHCP, Exchange, SQL Server, and so forth.

[82] Several such scenarios are highlighted here:
http://support.microsoft.com/kb/925652.

URL of which is indeed www.mynetwork.com, which mysteriously enough is accessible from anywhere except *your* network.

Recall that in our discussion of DNS, mention was made of the notion of an *authoritative DNS server*. In short, an authoritative DNS server is one that "knows" about a given domain (called *zone* in DNS-speak). The zone configuration defines what hostnames and IPs are known to exist for that domain. When the user tries to browse to the URL http://www.mynetwork.com, his/her computer does a DNS query to find the IP address associated with this resource name. Under normal circumstances, this would cause the machine to query whatever DNS server it is aware of (your local domain controller, in this case), which would then forward the request outside to a public DNS server (a process called *recursion*, as mentioned in Chapter 1). However, since you saw fit to name your internal Windows domain with the hapless designation mynetwork.com, the local domain controller and its DNS services think that *it* is the authoritative DNS server for this domain/zone. Since you do not have a web server running on your network, and since there is thus no resource record for the DNS server to provide back to the querying computer, the answer comes back as "I don't know," and the site is never found. Meanwhile, the same process completed outside the local network queries a different DNS server, which does its due diligence of recursion and finds the correct answer, thus allowing the site to be visited.

The moral of the story is this: when naming Windows domains, unless you or your organization have registered the domain name, it is best to use a *.local* suffix. Like the ranges of IP addresses that are *reserved* for private use, *.local* domains are never registered with public DNS, and so are not known outside your four walls.

7.9
Domains Members and Clients

In the context of Active Directory, a "client" is a computer that requests access to resources or information from another computer. This could be a workstation communicating with a server, or a server communicating with another server. In order to authenticate against Active Directory and use resources offered there, a user must have a valid set of credentials (login name and password). This user account object is then stored in Active Directory. However, account objects are not limited to users alone: a computer must also have an account, which is created and stored in Active Directory, and which identifies the machine (rather than the user) for security purposes.

A computer account is created when a Windows machine is *joined* to the domain. A user must have both local and domain administrator privileges to join the machine to the domain. Once joined, the computer is identified by its NetBIOS name (if NetBT is enabled), as well as its fully-qualified domain name (FQDN). A machine running the workstation version of Windows can become a member of the domain, but cannot host services like DNS or Active Directory. A machine running Windows Server 2000 or above is first joined as a member (if being added to an existing domain), and then may be promoted to domain controller and/or global catalog server. The distinction between *member servers* and domain controllers is thus established. A member server is a server that does not host Active Directory. (It may, however, host other services related to Active Directory, such as WINS or DNS.)

It is important to understand that both computers and users have Active Directory accounts. Though they perform different tasks, both are necessary for the domain to function properly. Should a member computer (workstation or server) have its account removed from Active Directory, it loses the ability to interact with the domain. The solution is often to simply re-join the domain—that is, run the wizard a second time with the same settings, thus recreating the computer account in Active Directory. If this does not resolve the issue, additional steps would be required, as determined by information gleaned from the event logs or other error messages that might appear.

7.10
Active Directory Administration

7.10.1
The Microsoft Management Console (MMC)

The MMC is the framework upon which management of a Windows 2000 and higher operating system is managed. Various *snap-ins* or modules are available for different tasks. The MMC is used for both machine-specific functions and domain- or forest-related administration. For example, the *Local Users and Groups* MMC is used to configure security accounts for a local machine (server or workstation), while the *Active Directory Users and Computers* MMC is used to manage user and computer accounts, security groups, and related objects within Active Directory.

In addition to the graphical interface of the MMC, command-line tools exist for administrative tasks related to Active Directory. In fact, some tasks are only possible from the command-line. An example of this is Ntdsutil.exe, a command-line utility used to "seize" the FSMO roles from a defunct domain controller and assigning them to another. In either case, depending on the task to be performed, an Administrator account (or a user with administrator privileges) is required.

7.10.2
"God Mode" (The Administrator Account)

In a Windows environment, there are actually three different "administrator" accounts: *Local Administrator*, *Domain Administrator*, and *Enterprise Administrator*. A local administrator has full rights over a local machine (client or server); as such, it exists on every Windows machine by default. Within an Active Directory domain environment, the domain administrator account has full rights over a given domain and its child domains, while the enterprise administrator account has rights over the entire forest.

7.10.2.1
Administrators Both Great and Small

Corresponding to the three administrator user accounts are three security groups with similar levels of power. The *Administrators* group on a given Windows machine has full rights over that machine, including the ability to add/change/delete users, install or uninstall software, and manage hardware. If the machine becomes a member of an Active Directory domain, the domain-level administrator group (*Domain Admins*) is added to the local *Administrators* group by default. This allows a user with domain administrator privileges to use the same account when managing domain resources or local machine resources on member machines. When a member server is promoted to become a domain controller, the Enterprise Admins group is also added to the local Administrators group on the server. Again, this provides a high-level administrator with full rights over the environment (from servers to forest) using the same login credentials.

Finally, if only one domain is configured within the forest (called the *root forest domain*, as mentioned above) the domain administrator account for that domain is also Enterprise Administrator for the Active Directory forest as a whole. Should additional domains be added subsequently, they can only be created by use of the Enterprise Administrator account or a different with the same privileges. The following diagram shows the relationship of the Administrator account at different levels of the XYZ Corporation forest. When logging into the system, the User Principal Name (UPN) format will be used to specify the domain (or child domain) in which the user account is stored. With this in mind, note that the root forest domain (xyz.local) has an administrator designated simply as *Administrator@xyz.local*. As an extreme example, since XYZ has seen fit to create multiple layers of domains and child domains, the domain Administrator account for the child domain named *marketing.west.xyz.local* would thus be referenced by the following unwieldy designation: *Administrator@marketing.west.xyz.local*.

Even more intimidating, however, is the LDAP Distinguished Name (DN):

CN=Administrator, DC=marketing, DC=west, DC=xyz, dc=local

Note, however, that an administrator of a higher-level domain has access over lower-level domains by default. This is because, as mentioned already, the admin group of the higher domain is automatically added to the "Domain Admins" group of the lower domain. For example, when the xyz.local forest was created, the Administrator account was created in the root-forest domain of the same name (xyz.local). When subsequent child domains are created within this forest, the administrator account of the root of the forest retains control over all objects created beneath it. Moreover, only users with Enterprise Administrator privileges (i.e., those who are members of the root-forest domain) can perform certain tasks, such as creating child domains. These considerations are important from an administrative standpoint (e.g., knowing what permissions are required for certain tasks), but also from a security standpoint (e.g., limiting access to this level of administrative power).

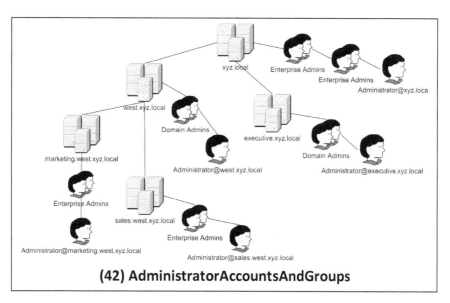

(42) AdministratorAccountsAndGroups

7.10.3
Active Directory Users and Computers

User and computer accounts are managed through the *Active Directory Users and Computers* MMC. Recall that both users and computers that are members of the domain have an account (security principal object) in Active Directory.

By default, a number of *containers* are created, into which objects are placed. The

Computers container contains known member machines. Domain controllers are placed into their own container. The Users container holds default accounts like Administrator, as well as default groups like Domain Admins. In addition to these default containers, Organizational Units (OUs) can be created for organizing users. An OU is a logical container that holds user accounts, groups, or machine accounts. For example, a Workstations OU might be created, into which all PCs are placed. The advantage of organizing Active Directory in this way is two-fold. First, it allows for a logical layout of objects, keeping like items together. Second, it allows for administrative tasks to be performed on multiple machine or user accounts simultaneously. By using a Group Policy Object (GPO), security and other policies can be automatically applied and enforced for a user, group, or machine.[83]

7.10.4
Managing Sites

Active Directory sites are managed through the *Active Directory Sites and Services* MMC snap-in. The screenshot below shows the interface. The *Subnets* container would include information about known IP subnets. Domain controllers configured under each site would be associated with a given subnet. Replication within each site occurs over the

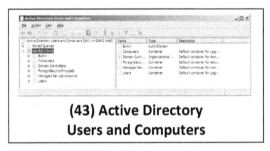

(43) Active Directory Users and Computers

LAN, while replication between sites is controlled by the *Inter-Site Transports* configuration. In the example below, there is a single *Site Link* connecting SiteA and SiteB. The *Cost* is a relative value that would prioritize multiple site links as higher or lower. The *Replication Interval* is the duration of time that passes between replication attempts. In this case, the replication is set to a 15-minute interval. Thus, if a user changes his or her password at SiteA, it will take up to 15 minutes for this change to be replicated to the DCs at SiteB.

---

[83]Group Policy is well outside the scope of this study. For more information, the reader is directed to the resources listed in the bibliography.

CHAPTER 8:
"BEWARE OF DOG!"
(THE KERBEROS PROTOCOL)

The previous sections of this study have focused on networking protocols and the topology (physical or logical) that supports them. The final two parts of this study will focus on two areas that are more related to security than networking *per se*. The present section provides an overview of the Kerberos protocol, a method of *authenticating*—that is, proving the identity of—a user or computer in an Active Directory domain. (This is to be distinguished from *authorization*, which controls what resources the authenticated user is able to access.) The final section offers a discussion of the administrator role in its varying degrees of authority in an Active Directory domain environment.

In Greek mythology, Kerberos (also spelled Cerberus) was a three-headed hound that guarded the gates of the Underworld (Hades) and kept the dead from returning to the realm of the living. Capturing it alive and without weapons became the 12th Labor of Heracles (a.k.a., Hercules), after which he was released from his labors.[84] In the world of computer networking, Kerberos is a security protocol that authenticates and authorizes access to resources. Objects such as user accounts, computer accounts, and security groups interact with Kerberos. In the case of computers, only systems running Windows 2000 are able to communicate with the protocol. In the case of users and groups, the specifics of Kerberos are behind-the-scenes, within the Active Directory domain itself.

The Kerberos protocol was developed at MIT to protect resources related to Project Athena, a joint effort of MIT, Digital Equipment Corporation, and IBM.[85] The goal of

---

[84]See http://en.wikipedia.org/wiki/Cerberus.

[85]Project Athena, named for the Greek goddess of wisdom, was responsible for creation of the X Window System—the first Graphical User Interface (GUI) for UNIX-based systems. It also

Project Athena was to create a campus-wide distributed computing environment. Thus, Kerberos was intended to protect network resources across multiple hosts. As adopted by Microsoft, Kerberos has been modified to use public key certificates rather than shared secret keys. This allows Kerberos to authenticate devices such as smart cards, as well as traditional user-provided passwords. The true power of Kerberos lies in its ability to perform *mutual authentication*—that is, to establish the identity of both the sender and receiver of a communication. This is different than single authentication, in which (for example) the sender provides credentials to prove its identity, but assumes that the receiver is trustworthy.

8.1
"Show Us Your Papers"

In order to communicate secretly, two entities must be able to identify the other as authentic. One method of doing so is a *shared secret*. For a simplistic example, suppose that two people wish to communicate in such a way that the identity of the sender is always verifiable. To accomplish this, they agree that the word "chocolate" will always be included in the message. Therefore, a message might end with a total *non sequitur*: "I really could use some chocolate today!" This proves that the sender is (or should be) identifying himself or herself with the shared secret, but it does nothing to hide the content of the actual message itself. It also opens up the possibility that a third party who intercepts enough messages will deduce that "chocolate" is the secret word, and be able to use this to some advantage.

To solve this problem, some method of masking the true meaning of the message is required. The Greek work *cryptos* means "hidden" or "secret," while *graphos* means "writing." *Cryptography* is the art and science of writing hidden messages; *encryption* is a method for writing the message to be unintelligible except to those "in the know." At its most simple, cryptography requires two things: a *cipher*[86] (some method by which the

---

influenced technologies such as thin computing, the Lightweight Directory Access protocol (LDAP), and instant messaging. See http://en.wikipedia.org/wiki/Project_Athena.

[86]The word *cipher* has an interesting etymology. The Arabic *sifr* (later Latin *cifra*) meant zero in the mathematical sense of the term. The concept of *zero* as a number was developed by Persian mathematicians during the Middle Ages. It was unknown to the West at this time, for the Roman numeral system had no such concept. Over time, it seems that the term "cipher" came to mean speaking in an unclear way, or concealment of clear messages. Meanwhile, the English language adopted the Italian word *zero* to mean no mathematical value (the number 0), but used the term *ciphering* for computing or calculating. Hence, the connotation of *cipher* as a means by which a

message is hidden) and a *key* (a piece of information necessary to *decipher* the message). A *cipher* can be as simple as letter substitution to turn an ordinary sentence into complete nonsense. *Cipher-text* refers to an encrypted message.

The user or computer account that is involved in a data communication is called a *Security Principal*. A *security principal* refers to an entity (an *object* in Active Directory) that can be positively identified by a technique called *authentication*. In order to be authenticated, the security principal must provide a *token*, some piece of data that uniquely identifies it amongst others that might look alike. For example, if you are pulled over by a police officer, among the first thing they ask for is a driver's license. In this case, *you* are the Security Principal, and the *token* you present is a state-issued motor vehicle operator's license. This license includes information about you (picture, height, weight, age, eye color), as well as a number that can be confirmed against a database. If all is well, the number on the license matches the record in the computer. You are therefore *authenticated*, that is, you are who you say you are.

In the case of a private conversation, however, this still leaves the question of how the information to be exchanged can be transmitted securely, so others cannot eavesdrop. The answer is *encryption*.

8.1.1
An Aside: A Short History of Secrets[87]

Cryptography has been around for centuries, and has changed greatly over the years. "Caesar's Cipher," so named because Roman Emperor Julius Caesar used it in ancient times to exchange coded communiqués with his generals, used a simple method of shifting each letter of forward or back by a number of spaces. For example, "A" in the original message might become "C" in the cipher-text. In order to *decrypt* the message, it would be necessary to know that the letters are shifted to the right by 2 spaces. This bit of information is known as the *key*, for it "unlocks" the cipher and allows the messaged to be read.

---

message was rendered hidden or secret came from a term that originally meant something having no value at all.

[87]We promise not to kill you afterward. ☺

By the 20th century, machines (such as the Enigma code machine used by the Nazis during World War II) had been invented that could do this type of work on a more sophisticated scale.[88] Other encryption types did not use a cipher *per se*, but simply relied on the ignorance of those who may be listening in. A classic example is the use of Native American languages, such as the Navajo dialect, that were unknown outside the tribe itself. So-called "Code Talkers" could speak to each other in Navajo over open airwaves without the enemy having the faintest idea of what they were saying![89]

Modern cryptography—that is, cipher methods developed since the close of WWII— are much different than those described above. So-called "classic" cryptography of the type used by Caesar or the Code Talkers was based on linguistics; a cryptographer of that era was a person of letters and languages. By contrast, the type of cryptography used in Kerberos and other modern computer systems is based on complex mathematical calculations called *algorithms*.[90] While the classic cryptographer might thus arise from the Humanities division of the university, his or her modern counterpart is a member of the Mathematics or Computer Science department.

English: A B C D E F G H I J K L M N O P Q R S T U V W X Y Z
Cipher: C D E F G H I J K L M N O P Q R S T U V W X Y Z A B
           Clear-text: SO MANY SECRETS
           Cipher-text: UQ OCPA UGETGVU

(44) Caesar's Cipher

---

[88]Looking like an ordinary typewriter, the Enigma machine used a series of rotors to transcribe ordinary text into complete gibberish. Only when several of the machines were captured by the Allies were they able to decrypt the messages being to and from Berlin. This history is the backdrop for the movie entitled *U-571*.

[89]This history became the backdrop for another Hollywood film entitled *Wind Talkers*.

[90]The term *algorithm* derives from the Latin form of a mathematician named Abū ʿAbdallāh Muḥammad ibn Mūsā al-Khwārizmī (try fitting that on a business card!), who lived in ancient Persia (that's modern-day Iran for those of you in Rio Linda). His most famous work, *The Compendious Book on Calculation by Completion and Balancing* includes in its Arabic title the word *al-ğabr*, one of two mathematical operations used in the book, from which we get our English word *algebra*. Latin translations of his works also introduced to the Western world the decimal placement systems, based on the Hindu-Arabic numbering (1,2,3...) that eventually replaced Roman numerals.

FOUNDATIONS OF WINDOWS NETWORKING

8.2
"Welcome to Baskerville.com.
This Site Requires Login"

8.2.1
The Three Heads of Kerberos

Like its mythological counterpart, Kerberos the computer protocol has three "heads" or roles by which it functions: a *client*, a *server*, and a trusted mediator called the *Key Distribution Center* (KDC). The KDC service runs on a Windows Server and maintains a database of information for the security protocols within its *realm* (the Kerberos equivalent of a domain). Included in this information is a cryptographic key known only to the security principal (user account, computer account, or group) and the KDC. The cryptographic key itself is calculated by applying an algorithm to the user's password. The resulting value is called a *long-term key*.

When a client requests access to resources on a server, the client sends a request first to the KDC for authentication. The KDC then issues a *short-term key* by which the two entities can authenticate each other (mutual authentication). It then sends the client both copies of session key, as follows:

- The client copy of the session key is encrypted using the long-term key that only they know. In this way, only the client can read the information provided by the KDC.
- The server copy of the session key, along with information about the client, is encapsulated into a data structure known as a *session ticket*. The session ticket is then encrypted with the long-term key that the KDC shares with the server.

Note that the client can read the first, but not the second, of these data units. Until it reaches the server, however, it is responsible for maintaining both parts, as they are required for the transaction about to take place. Note also that the KDC does not attempt to maintain a listing of what tickets were issues, nor ensure that they are delivered. The KDC simply acts as a ticket-issuance entity that then hands off this responsibility to another party (the client). This removes the burden that would otherwise be placed on the KDC to manage all of these connections and relationships, and allows it to run more efficiently. Nor is there a security risk in this regard, for only an entity possessing the client's secret key can decrypt the client copy of the session key, and likewise with the server's copy. Thus, were the encrypted session key to be intercepted by a third party, it could do nothing without the secret key needed to unlock the contents.

When the client receives the reply from the KDC, it extracts the session ticket (the contents of which it cannot read) and the client copy of the session key (which *is* able to decrypt) and stores them in a secure location in *volatile memory* (also called Random Access Memory, or RAM) and not on disk. To request access to the resources on the server, it then transmits a message containing two pieces of information:

- The session ticket, still encrypted with the server's private key.
- An authenticator, encrypted with the session key it received from the KDC.

Together, these two items serve as the credentials validating the client's identity. Only the KDC can issue the session ticket, the contents of which is readable only by the server, using the private key it shares with the KDC. Likewise, only the client can encrypt a message with its copy of the session key, as received from the KDC. Since the session key and session ticket match, this proves that the client request is coming from a valid source.

When the server receives this information, it decrypts the session ticket with its private key, extracts the session key, and then uses the session key to decrypt the authenticator as created by the client. These three are then compared, and if found to be valid, the server knows that the credentials provided were issued by the trusted third-party, the KDC. If the client has requested mutual authentication, this process is reversed: the server now uses its copy of the session key to encrypt the timestamp attached to the authenticator it received from the client. This is then returned to the client as an authenticator.

Throughout this process, the onus is on the client, not the server, to provide the credentials necessary to establish further communication. Each request made to the server from a particular server includes the session ticket received from the KDC. This allows the server to authenticate each new session independently. The server retains its private key for use with decryption of incoming requests, but when the session key is no longer needed, it is discarded. Likewise, when a KDC replies to a client request, it returns a session key for itself. This special version of the session ticket is called a *Ticket-Granting Ticket* (TGT), and functions much the same way as the session ticket. When the client receives this TGT, it decrypts the message using its copy of the session key, then discards the long-term key that was calculated from the user's password, as it is no longer needed. Instead, all further communication is done by using the session key. A session key used between a client and a KDC is called a *logon session key*, and is valid until the TGT expires or the user logs off, whichever comes first.

As already indicated, session tickets are reusable for a set time period, then expire. This means that the client is able to issue multiple requests against a server using the same credentials, without needing to contact the KDC. The *timeout* value after which a session ticket expires is controlled by the Kerberos policy on the domain, and stored in the session ticket itself. If the user logs off the system before that time, however, the credentials cache is flushed and all session tickets expire immediately. Since the session tickets and other KDC-provided information is held in volatile memory (RAM), there is no way to retrieve them once a flush of the memory has occurred.

The advantage of using a Ticket-Granting Ticket is the offloading of CPU and memory resources necessary to do the calculations involved. A lookup of the long-term key is done only when generating a TGT, after which the Key Distribution Center service can use the logon session key as the authenticator for further communications with the client.

8.2.2
Trust, but Verify

As mentioned above, *mutual authentication* refers to a process whereby both parties in the communication are identified by some trusted method. In the case of Kerberos, the method is the session keys and authenticators that are exchanged between the computers, security tokes that are issued by a trusted party (the KDC). Mutual authentication is critical to a network environment where information is exchanged over a medium (Ethernet) that does not itself provide a secure mode of transport. Data passing over the wire (or broadcast by the wireless system) is simply a stream of bits (0s and 1s). Should a nefarious third-party ("hacker") wish to intercept these transmissions, freely-available tools exist that can do just this.[91]

It is important to note that users of a network assume certain risks, especially if efforts have not been made to ensure that the shared medium is secured—that is, closed to unauthorized outsiders. Kerberos itself only provides a means of authenticating the various entities on the network against a shared, trusted directory. Once this authentication is complete, the means by which the data is exchanged is left to the protocols used. In most cases, transmissions on a private network (and even public Internet) are unencrypted. Kerberos does nothing to protect the exchange of data itself, only the authentication process of those sending or receiving the data.

8.3
Kerberos the Windows Way

The Key Distribution Center (KDC) is a domain service running on a domain controller (Windows 2000 or above). Both the KDC and Active Directory services are started by the Local Security Authority (LSA) service, which is responsible for managing security for that machine. KDC uses Active Directory as its account database, and the global catalog as its directory for user information. Thus, KDC is reliant upon a functioning Active Directory structure.

You might recall that the Active Directory (LDAP) service listens on TCP port 389. Kerberos, meanwhile, listens on UDP port 88. A client machine wishing to contact a KDC first executes a DNS lookup to find the SRV records that point to a local domain controller. Once found, the LSA on the local computer then sends a user datagram to port 88 on the IP address of the DC, and begins the process of authentication. All communiqués between client and KDC are encrypted using session key, thus ensuring that a third party is kept out of the loop. Leaving aside the complexity of the authentication process itself, the point to be remembered is that it is the Local Security Authority service on the local machine that interacts with the Key Distribution Center service on the remote

---

[91]The Wireshark (open source) and Microsoft Network Monitor tools are free "packet sniffer" (more appropriately named *protocol analyzer*) applications capable of reading and analyzing information from a network. In the absence of encryption, these frames and packets are *clear-text* and can easily be reassembled and parsed by the protocol analyzer.

machine (domain controller) and makes authentication possible.

8.3.1
Kerberos Provides "Authentication," *not* "Authorization"

A key distinction must be made between Kerberos as an authentication protocol and the other security protocols in Active Directory that provide access control (authorization) for resources. In short, Kerberos is the means by which the user or computer account is made known to the directory services. The act of logging into a Windows workstation computer using an Active Directory user account does not in-and-of itself *authorize* the user to do anything. What is provided, rather, is Ticket-Granting Ticket (TGT) by which session keys can be obtained for other services in the domain. As an analogy, suppose that there is a building with a front door, behind which is a small lobby area lined with more doors. Each door is locked and accessible only with a specific key (different for each). By authenticating at the front door, the user is identified as valid and permitted to enter the lobby; however, simply standing in the lobby accomplishes nothing of value. Without access to the resources (rooms) behind the additional doors, the user has done nothing more than authenticate to the system.

8.3.2
The Windows Logon Process

Anyone who has used a version of Windows NT or above is familiar with the welcome screen and its invitation to simultaneously press the *Control*, *Alternate*, and *Delete* keys (CTRL+ALT+DEL), after which the user is presented with a login screen. This key combination is known as the Secure Attention Sequence (SAS). By initiating the SAS, the user triggers a number of functions in the background. The first is that the *Netlogon* service (a program running the background on every Windows machine)[92] changes the screen to the logon desktop and then calls the *Graphical Identification and Authentication* (GINA), a component of the Netlogon service. It is the GINA that collects information such as username, password, and domain name from the user, wraps it within a data structure, and then forwards this information to the Local Service Authority (LSA) service. The LSA then sends the information on to the KDC, which queries Active Directory and the global catalog to confirm the user's identity. The reply sent from the KDC includes the Session Key and Session Ticket, which are send to the LSA and stored in memory (not on disk). Two things are now true: (1) the user is *authenticated* and (2) the computer possesses the

---

[92]The *Netlogon* service exists on both Window Server and desktop version of the operating system, and is responsible for the management of user login sessions.

necessary *security token* to request access (authorization) to network resources

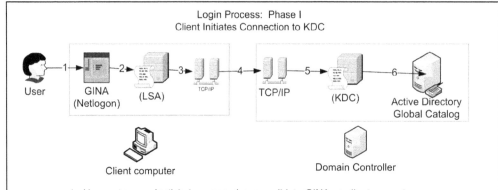

Login Process: Phase I
Client Initiates Connection to KDC

1 - User enters credentials (username/password) into GINA on client computer
2 - GINA sends information to LSA
3 - LSA sends data to TCP/IP stack, across network, to other computer
4 - TCP/IP stack on other computer parses frames and packets and passes data up to KDC
5 - KDC queries Active Directory and Global Catalog for information on user account

Login Process: Phase II
KDC Responds to Client

1 – Active Directory verifies that the Security Principal matches the user credentials presented to the KDC

2 – The KDC encapsulates the Session Key and Session Ticket and passes them to TCP/IP stack.

3 – The TCP/IP stack on the DC encapsulates the data into packets and frames and transmits the data to the TCP/IP stack of the client computer.

4 – The TCP/IP stack on the client computer parses the data and passes it to the LSA

5 – The LSA now possesses the session key and session ticket needed to authenticate to access other resources. These are stored in memory (not disk) on the client computer.

6 – The user is now authenticated. The Netlogon service calls the operating system to start a shell, which presents the user with an interface that utilizes their Windows profile.

(45) The Kerberos Logon Process

8.3.3
Kerberos and Windows File Sharing

Building on the previous example, let us say that the user has opened an application on his or her workstation. Within the application, a file is then opened. The file is physically located not on the local machine, but on a remote file server. The client computer, using the credentials and security token already received, is now able to request access to the file share where the data is located.

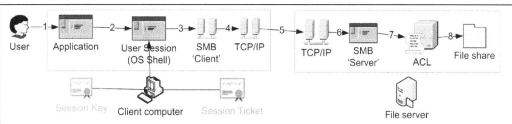

1 – User opens an application, then wishes to open a file from a share on the file server.

2 – The application is running under the user's account as part of their User Session, which is an instance of the operating system shell assigned to that user. As such, the Kerberos security credentials (authenticator) previously obtained is linked to the user session (OS shell) and any applications run on it.

3 – The application presents its request for data to the OS shell, which determines that the resource is remote and must be accessed via the network.

4 – Because the data to be retrieved is part of a Windows share, the OS shell hands off the request to the SMB (Server Message Block) 'client' service.

5 – The SMB message is passed to the TCP/IP stack, where it is encapsulated in an IP packet, which is then encapsulated in an Ethernet frame, and sent across the wire to the file server.

6 – The file server receives the frame and passes it through its TCP/IP stack, which presents the request to the SMB 'Server' service.

7 – Included in the data received by the file server's SMB Server service is the *authenticator* sent by the client, which the SMB Server uses to prove the client's identity. The user is now authenticated. The SMB Server then compares the credentials to the Access Control List attached to the Active Directory object of the file share. If the user account has at least Read Access to the file share, the request is *authorized* (granted).

(46) Kerberos Authentication Process

Those interested in more detail should consult the reference documentation.[93]

---

[93]See the Microsoft TechNet article on the Kerberos implementation in Windows Server 2000 and 2003/2003 R2: http://technet.microsoft.com/en-us/library/bb742431.aspx.

CHAPTER 9:
BASIC WINDOWS®
NETWORK ADMINISTRATION

The following section delves deeper into the world of networking specific to Windows Server. This is by no means a total overview of the responsibilities of server administration.

Before continuing to a deep-dive into Microsoft DNS services, mention should be made of the Berkley Internet Name Daemon (BIND), the original implementation of DNS services still widely used. Written for UNIX/Linux but also ported to Windows, BIND is the most popular DNS program in existence, and has stood the tests of time as the Internet has grown from a handful of systems hosted by universities to a global communications network.

Early versions of BIND stored DNS information in flat-files. The current implementation of BIND (version 9.x) was written from scratch a number of years ago, and supports a variety of database formats for storing zone information. By contrast, Microsoft DNS services were written (not surprisingly) by Microsoft, for use with its Windows operating system. Microsoft DNS can operate in one of two modes: Active Directory Integration, in which DNS information is stored in Active Directory, or standalone, in which data is stored outside of AD. Because non-Windows clients can make use of the DNS services as well, there is really no advantage to not configuring them together for a Windows network.[94]

---

[94]The possible exception would be a Windows Server used to host DNS for the public Internet. In this case, security concerns might dictate that a standalone server (i.e., part of a workgroup rather than the domain) be used to host DNS, which would then also be standalone.

9.1
DNS Manager

The Microsoft DNS Service is managed using the DNS Manager snap-in for the Microsoft Management Console (MMC). DNS Manager is accessible from the Administrative Tools menu on a domain controller, or via command-line as **dnsmgmt.msc**. By default, a connection to the local domain controller is established automatically, though other domain controllers can be added to the view, as shown below.

The DNS Manger represents the DNS records it maintains as a hierarchy of folders and subfolders. At the top is DNS, representing the root of the DNS service itself. Listed here are the DNS servers that have been added to the view. Below this is

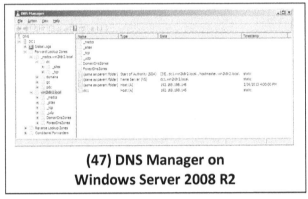

**(47) DNS Manager on
Windows Server 2008 R2**

an entry for each DNS server individually, beneath which is the structure of records being held by that server.

9.2
AD and DNS: Dependencies and Requirements

Especially in small networks, it is common (and best) practice to install the DNS service onto one or more of the domain controllers in the network.[95] This design reduces the number of servers and simplifies the configuration. Certain dependencies also come into play when designing the Active Directory structure of an organization. First, installation of Active Directory requires DNS. Before AD can be configured on a server (using the **dcpromo** command), DNS services must be installed and available for use. The wizard often does this along the way, but certain versions of Windows require that these services or roles be installed in advance of running **dcpromo** to create a domain controller.

---

[95]A scenario under which a Windows server that is not a domain controller might be configured for DNS services is an organization that wants to host DNS for public-facing (externally-accessible) websites or applications. By placing these records on a separate (and isolated) DNS server, security risks for internal systems are minimized.

Second, Active Directory Integration is only available when DNS and AD are running on the same machine. Active Directory Integration is an option whereby DNS information is stored in Active Directory itself, rather than in a separate database. This is the default/recommended practice, and has certain advantages. Clients that are joined to the domain can be automatically registered with DNS, and have those registrations updated as needed. The **ipconfig/registerdns** command allows a client machine (workstation or member server) on the domain to register its hostname and IP address with the DNS server. This information is stored in Active Directory, and so the correlation between the hostname and IP address of the node and the Active Directory computer account is established automatically. Additionally, since Active Directory automatically replicates between domain controllers at the same or different sites, DNS information is also replicated along with this process.

9.3
Zones and Records

DNS is divided into *zones*, which correspond to a given Top-Level Domain (TLD). The first zone created is for the local domain, in this case, hisc.local. Note that it is not signified in any way differently from the other zones. This is because as far as DNS is concerned (at least at this level), all zones are the same. Zones are referred to as either **Forward Lookup** or **Reverse Lookup**, depending on their function. Within each zone, various types of records are stored. Each type of record has a specific purpose, as will be outlined below. Before launching into the zone types, however, a description of a specific type of record is in order: the Start of Authority (SOA).

9.3.1
Start of Authority (SOA) Records

"One lookup zone to rule them all,
One SOA to find them,
One "A" (host) record to register
and in the zone files BIND them!"

The Start of Authority (SOA) record is the first resource record created in a DNS zone, and can be . The SOA contains information about the zone. The following information applies to an Internet DNS zone, but is also largely applicable to the Microsoft DNS service as configured for a Windows domain.

155

1. **Source host**: The host server (DC) where the file was created.
2. **Contact email**: Contact information for the person responsible for administering the zone. Note that a dot is used in place of the @ sign.
3. **Serial number**: This value should be incremented with each change to the DNS records within the zone. By incrementing the serial number, peer or secondary DNS servers are made aware that changes have been made that must be replicated or propagated accordingly.[96]
4. **Refresh Time**: Measured in seconds, this is the time a secondary DNS server will wait before issuing a query against the primary DNS server's SOA record, in order to check for changes. When the refresh time expires, the secondary DNS server(s) request a new copy of the SOA record from the primary DNS server. The response received is then compared to the existing record. If the serial number in the existing record does not match the new SOA record just received, the secondary DNS server requests a *zone transfer*. (More on this concept below.)
5. **Retry Time**: Measured in seconds, the time a secondary DNS server waits before retrying a failed zone transfer. The retry time is usually less than the refresh interval, such that a zone transfer that was initiated but not completed can be retried before another SOA record is requested, thus starting the whole cycle over again.
6. **Expire Time**: Measured in seconds, the time during which the secondary DNS server will keep retrying the zone transfer. If no successful transfer is completed before the expire time, the secondary DNS server will stop answering queries, since its records are deemed incomplete or inaccurate.
7. **Minimum Time-to-Live (TTL)**: Measured in seconds, the Time-to-Live is applied to all records, and informs secondary servers how long the record should be held in cache before an update is requested from the primary server.

NOTE: Microsoft DNS services allow these values to be stored as minutes, hours or even days!

9.3.1.1
SOA and Zone Transfers

A *zone transfer* is the process by which the contents of a DNS zone are copied from a primary DNS server to a secondary DNS server. Because of the nature of Windows networking, however, transfer zones are not applicable. Rather, following best practices, a Windows domain should include DNS servers that are (likely) also domain controllers,

---

[96]In a Windows domain environment, this incrementing is done automatically.

with Active Directory integration storing DNS information within AD. Nonetheless, because Microsoft's DNS services are a full implementation of DNS that is compatible with non-Windows clients, an understanding of these basics can be helpful when troubleshooting issues.

9.3.2
Forward Lookup Zones

A **Forward Lookup Zone** contains DNS records that resolve a hostname or Fully-Qualified Domain Name to an IP address. A forward lookup zone is created for each domain for which the DNS server has been made authoritative. (Recall that an authoritative DNS server is one that holds records for a given domain, and thus "knows" about that domain. Other servers then query this DNS server for information about that domain.)

9.3.2.1
A Records

An A record ("A" for Address) points to the IP address of a host, thus resolving a hostname to an IP. A records are used for a number of query types, such as remote access programs, file shares, and so forth.

9.3.2.2
Alias (CNAME) Record

Unlike an A record, an Alias or CNAME record does not point to an IP address, but rather to an A record. A CNAME allows DNS to record an alternate name for a host or IP address that is linked to the actual A record. Obviously, it would be possible to simply create another A record, with another name pointing to the same IP. The advantage of a CNAME is that if the original/actual A record to which it is pointed should change, the CNAME follows with it. This makes administration of the CNAME record a "set and forget" process.

9.3.2.3
Mail Exchanger (MX) Record

A Mail Exchanger or MX record points to a host that is providing email services.

Specifically, an MX record points to a server that is running the SMTP protocol, which usually runs on port TCP 25. Messages sent to the IP address listed in the MX record should therefore be accepted by the SMTP service on the server in question.

9.3.2.4
Name Server (NS) Record

Name Server records, as the name indicates, point to DNS servers. When a Windows workstation that has been added to a domain comes online, part of the startup process is to query the network for an available DNS server. The Name Server is then used to query for other record types (detailed below) that inform the workstation as to the location of other resources, such as an Active Directory Domain Controller.

9.3.2.5
Service Records (SRV)[97]

As the name implies, a Service Records provide information about services running on the network. When a Domain Controller (DC) starts up, it registers the services it is running with DNS in the form of SRV records. Other Windows machines on the network then use DNS to query for this information and find the services being offered by the DC(s).

Active Directory is an implementation of LDAP. Thus, if a workstation or member server needs to find a Domain Controller for domain xyz.local, it issues a DNS query for a record with the form of **_ldap._tcp.xyz.local**. (Underscores are used to prevent confusion with other names in the namespace.)

9.3.2.5.1
Global Catalong (_gc)

Global Catalog service records point to a domain controller that has been configured as a Global Catalog. The following information is stored in this record:

1. **Domain**: The domain in which it has been created.

---

[97]The following discussion of Service Records is far from exhaustive. For more information on the SRV records, see http://technet.microsoft.com/en-us/library/cc961719. Though written for Windows 2000, the concepts and data types remain consistent across subsequent versions.

2. **Service**: The type of service being offered (GC for Global Catalog in this example).

3. **Protocol**: TCP or UDP

4. **Priority**: A number assigned to the record to designate its priority relative to other records of the same type. Clients always attempt to contact the server that reports the lowest priority number.

5. **Weight**: The number assigned here is used for load-balancing among target servers bearing the same priority assignment. Clients first try to find the lowest priority server. If multiple servers are located with the same priority, the client randomly chooses one from the group. Assigning different weight designations to different servers with the same priority would allow an administrator to direct traffic to specific servers (such as if older and new machines were in use during an upgrade).

6. **Port Number**: The TCP or UDP port number used by the service being hosted. Most services have standard ports that will be automatically configured during setup, and should not be altered.

7. **Host offering this service**: The fully-qualified domain name (FQDN) of the server to which the SRV record is pointed. In small environments, the same server probably hosts all services (i.e., domain controller, global catalog, DNS). All records will thus point back to this same FQDN. Larger networks might separate these roles, however, such that a DNS server is not also domain controller or Global Catalog.

9.3.2.5.2
_kerberos

The _*kerberos* SRV record points to the Kerberos authentication service running on a Domain Controller. As discussed above (see Chapter 8), Kerberos is the protocol that is responsible for authenticating users or computers in order to grant them access to network resources.

9.3.2.5.3
_ldap

The _*ldap* SRV record points to the Lightweight Directory Access Protocol (LDAP) services running on a domain controller. Active Directory is an implementation of LDAP. When a workstation requires information from the directory, it therefore queries DNS in order to locate an available LDAP/AD service and the domain controller that is hosting it.

9.3.3
Reverse Lookup Zones

Reverse lookup zones are named automatically using the subnet with which they are associated [subnet].in-addr-arpa. Note that the subnet is listed in reverse order. For example, a reverse lookup zone for IP subnet 192.168.1.0/24 would be created as *1.168.192.in-addr.arpa* in Windows DNS.

9.3.3.1
Reverse Lookup (PTR) Records

In simple terms, a PTR (pointer) record points (hence the name) to an IP address to a hostname. This is called a *reverse lookup*, because it does the exact opposite of what an A record does (pointing a hostname to an IP address). Reverse lookups are helpful when resolving hostnames and IPs on a network, especially when troubleshooting issues. The important thing to remember is that A (host) and PTR records must match! The screenshot below shows the PTR record for a workstation.

9.3.4
A Zone Apart: "_msdcs"

If you spend any time at all perusing a DNS server configured for Active Directory integration (usually hosted on a domain controller), you will notice that aside from the expected zone information for the domain, another series of folders appear as well, bearing the strange prefix *_msdcs*. Thus you have uncovered one of the hidden marvels of Windows networking: the symbiotic relationship between DNS and Active Directory. ☺

When a Windows server is configured as a domain controller (using the **dcpromo** command), the Active Directory installer creates a DNS forward lookup zone named for the forest being created. A subdomain within this zone is also created, named _msdcs.*ForestName*.[98] Figure 67 below shows the entries on a DNS server hosting records for a root-forest domain named win2008r2.local. Note that the subdomain record has been created with the name *_msdcs.win2008r2.local*.

The _msdcs subdomain and its records were first introduced in Windows 2003, as a method by which a domain controller could be more easily found on the network.

---

[98] Since you are no-doubt curious, _msdcs is a an acronym (and who didn't expect that?) for Microsoft Domain Controller Service.

(Subsequent versions of Windows, i.e., Server 2008 and Server 2008R2, also include this methodology.) These changes make the subdomain that is linked to the domain a more Windows-specific. In short, records associated with the subdomain _msdcs.win2008r2.local_ given in the example above would allow client machines to more easily find Windows-specific services, by pointing the Net Logon service (the backend of the user login process) to the appropriate SRV records in DNS. The SRV record then points the client to the appropriate IP address and port number from which the service being requested is hosted.[99]

9.4
Root Hints

Root hints are files containing information about root DNS on the public Internet. When DNS is first installed, root hints are created on the server. It is possible to update them thereafter, based on new information available from the Internet. The purpose of root hints is to present a "last-option" for DNS queries that are otherwise unanswerable. For example, suppose that a client machine requests the IP address of xyz.com. The local DNS server is not authoritative, and so tries to do a lookup. How will it know the address of another DNS server? Barring other means (see section below), it will use the root hints to contact a top-level DNS server on the Internet. Note, however, that this is not the preferred means, since these root DNS servers are not intended to be queried in this fashion. Microsoft rather provides for a different means by which our conscientious local DNS server can obtain the information it needs: _DNS forwarding_.

9.5
DNS Forwarding

As the name implies, a DNS Forwarder entry points a DNS server to other (usually external and/or public) DNS servers. DNS forwarding thus allows a non-authoritative DNS server to pass a query along to another server, and onto another and another until an authoritative server is found that can answer the query. DNS Forwarder entries are universal, and used by all clients (without their knowledge) when the local DNS server

---

[99] For an exhaustive explanation of DNS and its relationship to Active Directory, see the following TechNet article: http://technet.microsoft.com/en-us/library/cc759550.aspx

does a recursive lookup to answer a query for which it is not authoritative.

9.5.1
Forwarders (Windows 2000 & 2003/2003 R2)

A *DNS Forwarder* is a record that points the local DNS server to outside resources. As mentioned above, the use of Forwarders is preferable to relying on root hints. Note, however, that the Windows 2008 R2 interface allows for root hints to be used of no forwarder records are configured.

The examples below depict Forwarder records pointing to other Windows Servers on the internal domain. For normal deployments, these records would instead point to public DNS servers, usually those provided by the ISP. If an IP is entered to create the Forwarder record, the Server FQDN field is automatically populated by doing a reverse lookup. Likewise, if the DNS hostname is entered, the IP is determined by A record lookup. If the reverse lookup zone is not configured, or the PTR record is not available, the hostname will not be populated.

9.5.2
Conditional Forwarders

In addition to the global DNS forwarder entries, a second type of record was introduced with Windows Server 2008. A *conditional forwarder* points queries for a given domain name to a specific set of DNS servers for resolution. The DNS servers used for these queries can thus be different than those used for other queries. This is effectively an exception to the rule created for all other domains.

An example of why this would be helpful is if two Windows root-forest domains exist within the same organization, each of which maintain their own DNS. By configuring conditional forwarding on both sides, pointing to each other, the systems on either domain can resolve hostnames in the other domain name. Thus, xyz.local and abc.local, though completely separate, can cross-resolve DNS queries by forwarding requests to the appropriate DNS server, in this case, *each other's*. All other queries would then be forwarded out to public DNS servers for resolution.

To create a Conditional Forwarder, right-click on the Conditional Forwarders container in the DNS MMC and choose new Conditional Forwarder. A screen then appears asking for the relevant information, and options as to where the data should be stored. The following screen shot depicts a Conditional Forwarder configured for the test.local domain. Note that without the conditional forwarder, queries against the test.local domain (a separate root-forest Windows domain) would fail, since the local DNS for win2k8r2.local has no records for this other domain, nor would the public DNS servers to which it would forward the query.

9.6
Microsoft DHCP Services

Microsoft DHCP Services, installable on a machine running the Windows Server operating system, are controlled by the Microsoft Management Console with the DHCP snap-in. The console can be access under Administrative Tools on the Start menu. Once opened, the console will connect to the local server by default. As of Windows 2008, DHCP services support both IPv4 and IPv6. Since IPv4 is commonly used on internal networks, the following examples demonstrate this functionality.

By default, Server Options are set automatically if the DHCP role is enabled on a domain controller. For example, Options **006 DNS Servers** and **015 DNS Domain Name** are automatically set to the loopback IP (127.0.0.1) and domain (win2k8r2.local) in the example below:

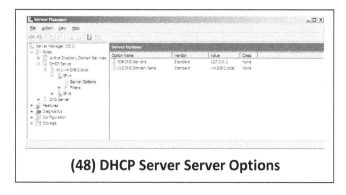

(48) DHCP Server Server Options

9.6.1
Creating and Naming a Scope

To create a DHCP scope, right-click on **IPv4** and choose **New Scope**. Click **Next** through the initial screen, and you arrive at the **Scope Name**. Here a name must be assigned to the scope. This can be alphanumeric, but should be descriptive enough to distinguish it from others that might follow. For the purposes of this example, the name

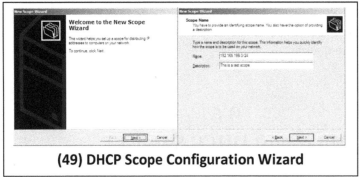

(49) DHCP Scope Configuration Wizard

of the scope is its subnet written in CIDR notation.[100]

9.6.2
Assign the DHCP Scope IP Range

On the screen that follows, the range of IPs to be used for the DHCP scope must be entered. Note that when you enter an IP address into the **Start IP address** box, the **Length** and **Subnet mask** fields below are automatically populated.[101]

For purposes of example, we have chosen the **192.168.199.0** subnet with a CIDR of **/24** (subnet mask 255.255.255.0). This will provide a block of addresses starting at 192.168.199.1 and ending at 192.168.199.254.

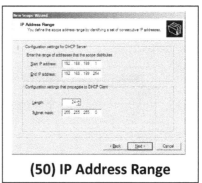

(50) IP Address Range

9.6.2.1
Address Exclusions and Server Delay

If any IP addresses must be excluded from the scope, they can be entered manually on the next screen. Exclusions, as the name imply, are exceptions to the rules being established by creating the DHCP scope. Thus, if you have an address range of 192.168.218.100 through 192.168.218.200, the system will assign IPs to clients starting with the first number and continuing until all IPs are assigned. Suppose, however, that a

---

[100]For a refresher on this acronym, see Section 2.4.3, "The Utopia of a 'Classless' Network."

[101]The system assumes that a Class C network (CIDR designation /24) is being used. If this is incorrect, manually adjusting the CIDR notation or Subnet mask field will change the settings accordingly. Again, a Class C or CIDR /24 subnet is often used for internal subnets (especially on smaller networks), so this setting is may not need any modification.

printer or other network device is discovered to have IP 192.168.218.50. Since this number falls within the range of the scope, the DHCP server may attempt to assign it to a client, thus creating an IP conflict situation on the network. When there is a conflict, either the static-assigned device or the DHCP-assigned device will stop functioning (and possibly both), and a Windows or other OS will probably display an error that the IP conflict has been detected. To avoid this situation, add the

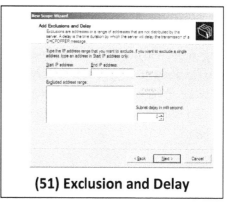

(51) Exclusion and Delay

appropriate IP(s) to the exclusion list. This tells DHCP to skip those IPs, even though they fall within its scope, and not attempt to assign them to a client.

9.6.3
Configure the Lease Duration

The duration of the scope determines how long an IP address assigned to a client is valid. When the lease expires, the client must request a new address. The length of the lease should be determined by considering several factors, such as:

1. The size of the network (larger vs. smaller).
2. The type of clients (laptops that may come and go, vs. desktops that are always connected).

For networks with relatively-static usage (i.e., the same computers are on the network most of the time), the lease time may be longer. For networks on which laptop or other mobile devices come and go, long lease times may become an issue, since devices will want to "remember" the number IP assigned. If the device fails to request a new address, and the existing address has since been assigned to another device, a conflict will occur. The default setting configured by Windows is 8 days, which seems to work well for most installations.

Finally, the subnet delay allows this server to wait for a time (in milliseconds) before answering DHCP client requests. This setting is only applicable to environments where multiple DHCP servers have been configured, and where the administrator wishes

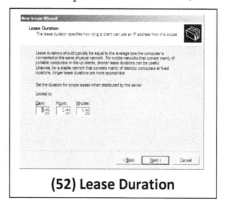

(52) Lease Duration

to control which server receives more or less traffic. For example, suppose that a network were being configured with an older and newer DHCP server. It would be possible with this setting to set a delay of X milliseconds on one machine, thus causing the DHCP requests to be answered by another server. Such a situation might arise if older and newer hardware were involved, and the legacy gear was being overloaded with requests. Note, however, that setting a delay is different from the concept of splitting the scope, to be discussed later.

9.6.3.1
Configure Scope Options

In addition to an IP address and subnet mask, a computer needs to know other

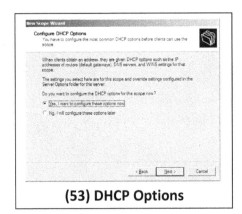

(53) DHCP Options

information about the network, such as the default gateway, location of DNS or WINS servers, and so forth. For machines with static IPs, these settings are configured as part of the setup. For DHCP clients, the settings are inherited from a standardized configuration that is pushed to the client after the IP address is assigned. These settings are called DHCP Scope Options, and are configured once per-scope.

By choosing to configure scope options before making the scope active, the basic settings can be assigned automatically to client devices, without need for manual intervention thereafter. For a Windows network (using Windows 2008 R2 in this example), various options the DHCP scope wizard prompts for certain types of information, as shown below in the order of their appearance:

9.6.3.2
Router (Default Gateway)

The default gateway is the IP of the device that connects the local subnet to others, including the Internet. For small networks, communications between internal systems can be done without specifying a default gateway. However, if a device wants to communicate with the Internet, it must know the default gateway by which this communication can be established.

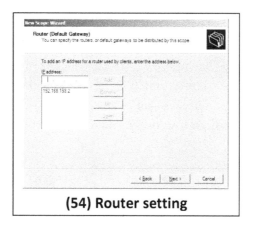

(54) Router setting

9.6.3.3
Domain Name and DNS Servers

The screen that follows may auto-populate the parent domain (Active Directory) and IP address of the DNS server(s) for that domain. Otherwise, these settings are manually entered. It is possible to add additional domains for the clients to search for DNS name resolution. For example, the domain **test.local** (used in the DNS Conditional Forwarders example above) can be set here as a default value. To add a domain to the list, enter the servername (FQDN) of the DNS server on the other domain and click Resolve, or enter the IP address of the DNS server and click Add. Windows will validate the address and if this test passes, add the IP to the list.

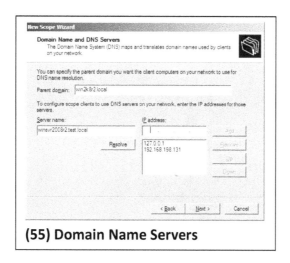

(55) Domain Name Servers

9.6.3.4
WINS Servers

NOTE: Though Windows 2000 included WINS for backward compatibility, recent versions of Windows desktop OS do not normally need or even use it. As a result, it is possible not to configure WINS services on a network comprised of Windows XP/Vista/7 clients, and thus, not to need a setting in the DHCP scope options pointing to these services.

(56) WINS Settings

9.6.4
Activate the Scope

Finally, the wizard asks if the scope should be activated. Activation is required if the scope is to begin servicing client devices. However, if settings are not fully-configured, then activation is not required at this point. (One reason not to activate right away might be to configure additional scope options not accounted for in the wizard screens.)

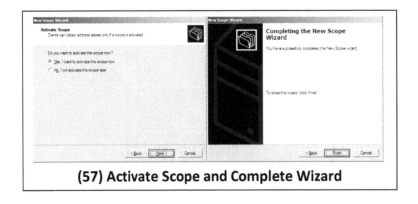

(57) Activate Scope and Complete Wizard

9.6.5
Reviewing the Settings

Once configured, the new DHCP scope appears in the MMC under its respective IP version (IPv4 in this case). Expanding the folders, we see that the various settings for this scope, as well as a folder named Server Options. Server Options are global to the DHCP setup, and apply to all domains. (As a result, this is *not* the place to assign a default gateway, since this is probably different for each subnet on a routed network. It would, however, be a convenient place to configure the DNS and other options that are universal for all clients.)

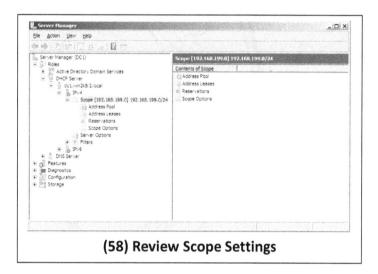

(58) Review Scope Settings

APPENDIX A:
NETWORKING "DO" AND "DON'T" LIST

A.1
DO...

- Connect all nodes/stations to an Ethernet switch instead of a hub. This isolates each node onto its own broadcast domain and allows for more efficient use of available bandwidth. (This is not really a challenge, as hubs are no longer manufactured.)
- Document your work, both as an aid in troubleshooting and a reference for future changes or upgrades.
- Make backups of configurations (or document the original settings) *before* modifying them.

A.2
DO NOT...

- Create a physical wiring loop between 2 ports on the same switch or router, as this will create a *broadcast storm*.
- Name internal domains with public domain names (use .local, not .com, .net) unless you own the domain name and have it properly registered!
- Allow inanimate objects to rule your life. When in doubt, ask for help and/or walk away for a while. (Technology is your *tool*, not your *master*.) ☺
-

APPENDIX B:
THE INS AND OUTS OF ETHERNET PORTS

When speaking of inbound or outbound traffic on a given network interface, the terms *ingress* and *egress* are sometimes used in technical documentation. *Ingress* refers to packets flowing into the device on that particular port or interface. *Egress*, logically enough, refers to packets flowing outbound from that interface. Managed devices such as enterprise-grade switches or routers are capable of providing statistics based on ingress/egress for the interfaces on the device, and thus can provide network monitoring software with usage data. Such information is helpful for troubleshooting purposes, such as in isolating a problem with the network, whereby a given interface may be overburdened or misconfigured. Longer term, this data is aggregated and used for trend analysis and forecasting, so network design can be modified as needed to meet the load expected.

(Next time you are at a party, or just in casual everyday usage, try throwing these terms around a bit and see what reaction you get. For example, instead of making a big entrance, you might want to *ingress* through the back door when arriving late for the staff meeting. Likewise, it is sometimes necessary to *egress* your desk or office in the direction of the coffee station or vending machine about mid-afternoon, as the day's fatigue begins to wear on. ☺)

APPENDIX C:
WIRING TYPES AND TERMS

The wire used for telephone and Ethernet networking, referred to as *Unshielded Twisted Pair* (UTP) appears similar from physical appearance, but functions somewhat differently. First, UTP refers to the fact that the wires (arranged in *pairs*) are twisted together and then covered with an outer sheathing. One or more pairs are then used to send and receive electrical signals. Wire is designated by a category (CAT) number, each of which supports a given range of signal frequencies (bandwidth) appropriate for different purposes. The higher the category number, the broader this range, but the more expensive the cabling.

CAT3   Used for analog phones and modems (*not* for computer networking!)
CAT5   Used for computer networks of 10Mbps or 100Mbps speeds (*not* Gigabit)
CAT5e   "Enhanced" Cat5 is used for Ethernet networks up to 1Gbps (Gigabit)
CAT6   Cat6 supports speeds up to 10Gbps (10-Gigabit over copper)

APPENDIX D:
MULTI-HOMING

(In case you were wondering, this chapter is not about that lakeside cabin you've been dreaming about.)

Under normal circumstances, a server or PC is connected to a single network or subnet. The term for this is *single-homed*. Conversely, a server or PC that is connected to multiple networks or subnets is called, conveniently enough, *dual-homed* or *multi-homed*. The physical equipment used to accomplish this configuration will vary depending on the network topology. For example, since a single NIC can be assigned more than one IP address, it would be possible for a server or PC to be dual-homed but have only 1 physical NIC. Conversely, a machine may have multiple NICs that work together to form a single, larger connection pool. This involved a concept called *NIC teaming*, a configuration made possible with special software.[102]

Dual- or multi-homed servers are usually configured for specific reasons, e.g., as firewalls or other special-purpose devices. Security best practices dictate that unless such a configuration is warranted, a single-home configuration should be used. This precludes, for example, the possibility that a "backdoor" could be created on the network. For example, suppose a server is connected to a firewall on Subnet A, but to the internal network on Subnet B. Under this scenario, an attacker able to compromise the dual-homed computer would have access to both subnets, and thus, potentially to all other computers on the network! This could be mitigated with firewalls or other security devices/configurations, but must be taken into account when designing the system.

---

[102] Servers often include a program that allows NICs to be *bound* or *trunked* together. NIC teaming also employs special protocols, such as Server Load Balancing (SLB) or the Link Aggregation Control Protocol (LACP), which must be supported and configured by both the NICs in the endpoint device (server or PC) and the networking gear (switches, routers) to which they are connected. NIC teaming can also be used to create high-bandwidth connections between network devices themselves, with the same rules applicable.

BIBLIOGRAPHY

NOTE: The following resources have been compiled during the writing of this study, but are not meant to be exhaustive. Sites such as Microsoft TechNet and Download Center should be consulted for the latest (free!) information on Microsoft products:

http://technet.microsoft.com/en-us/
http://www.microsoft.com/download/en/default.aspx

Active Directory

Windows Server 2003
Active Directory Operations Guide:

http://www.microsoft.com/downloads/en/details.aspx?FamilyID=6a238df8-115c-4e1a-89f1-ee9bc9486c0f&DisplayLang=en

Active Directory Backup/Recovery

http://technet.microsoft.com/en-us/library/cc771290%28WS.10%29.aspx
Applies to: Windows Server 2000, Windows Server 2003, Windows Server 2003 R2

http://technet.microsoft.com/en-us/library/cc771290%28WS.10%29.aspx
Applies to: Windows Server 2008, Windows Server 2008 R2:

Active Directory General Overview

http://technet.microsoft.com/en-us/library/cc758535%28WS.10%29.aspx

HOWTO: Seize FSMO Roles

http://support.microsoft.com/kb/255504

HOWTO: Transfer FSMO Roles

http://support.microsoft.com/kb/324801

HOWTO: Verify an Active Directory Install

Windows Server 2000: http://support.microsoft.com/kb/298143/EN-US/

Windows Server 2003: http://support.microsoft.com/kb/816106/en-us

Windows Server 2008 & 2008 R2
Active Directory Domain Services

http://technet.microsoft.com/en-us/library/cc770946%28WS.10%29.aspx

Address Resolution Protocol (ARP)

http://www.osischool.com/lesson-store

Networking terminology

Internet Control Message Protocol (ICMP)

http://en.wikipedia.org/wiki/Internet_Control_Message_Protocol

OSI Model

http://en.wikipedia.org/wiki/OSI_model
http://www.erg.abdn.ac.uk/users/gorry/eg3561/road-map.html

Dynamic Host Configuration Protocol (DHCP)

http://en.wikipedia.org/wiki/Dynamic_Host_Configuration_Protocol

Domain Names Space and the Domain Name Service

Top-Level Domains

http://www.icann.org/en/tlds/

Root DNS Servers

http://en.wikipedia.org/wiki/Root_nameserver

Domain Name System Overview

http://en.wikipedia.org/wiki/Domain_Name_System

DNS and Active Directory

Technet: "How DNS Support for Active Directory Works"
http://technet.microsoft.com/en-us/library/cc759550.aspx

DNS "Root Hints"

Technet: http://technet.microsoft.com/en-us/library/cc958982.aspx
Applies to: Windows Server 2000 and above

Technet: http://technet.microsoft.com/en-us/library/cc757965%28WS.10%29.aspx
Applies to: Windows Server 2003 and Windows Server 2003 R2

Group Policy Objects (GPO)

"Group Policy Settings Reference for Windows and Windows Server"
http://www.microsoft.com/download/en/details.aspx?id=25250

"Information on new Group Policy preferences in Windows 2008"
http://support.microsoft.com/kb/943729

Introduction for Windows Server 2003:
http://www.microsoft.com/download/en/details.aspx?id=14392

Introduction for Windows Server 2008:
http://kb.mit.edu/confluence/display/ist/Windows+Server+Platforms+-
+Introduction+to+Group+Policy

Kerberos

http://technet.microsoft.com/en-us/library/bb742431.aspx

Applies to: Windows Server 2000, Windows Server 2003, Windows Server 2003 R2

http://technet.microsoft.com/en-us/library/cc749438.aspx

Applies to: Windows Vista, Windows Server 2008 Enhancements

http://technet.microsoft.com/en-us/library/dd560670.aspx
Applies to: Windows 7, Server 2008 R2 Enhancements

Network Address Translation(NAT)

http://en.wikipedia.org/wiki/Network_address_translation

NetBIOS (over TCP/IP)

The Computer Browser Service

http://support.microsoft.com/kb/188001
Applies to: Windows 2000, Windows XP

Troubleshooting the Browser Service

http://support.microsoft.com/kb/188305
Applies to: Windows Server 2000, Windows Server 2003:

Network Time Protocol (NTP)

U.S. Navy/Naval Observatory

U.S. Department of the Navy Time Service Department: http://tycho.usno.navy.mil/

U.S. Naval Observatory Master Clock: http://tycho.usno.navy.mil/mc_to.html

U.S. Naval Observatory NTP Servers: http://tycho.usno.navy.mil/ntp.html

The NTP Pool Project homepage

http://www.pool.ntp.org/en

Server Message Block (SMB)

Opportunistic Locking (SMB v1 only): http://support.microsoft.com/kb/296264

TCP and UDP

TCP overview

http://en.wikipedia.org/wiki/Transmission_Control_Protocol
http://technet.microsoft.com/en-us/library/cc778264%28WS.10%29.aspx

UDP overview

http://en.wikipedia.org/wiki/User_Datagram_Protocol

Windows Firewall

"Introduction to Windows Firewall with Advanced Security"
 http://www.microsoft.com/download/en/details.aspx?id=19192
Applies to: Windows Vista, Windows 7, Windows Server 2008/2008 R2

Windows Server Technology Collections

The Microsoft TechNet Library:
 http://technet.microsoft.com/en-us/library/bb625087.aspx

www.ingramcontent.com/pod-product-compliance
Lightning Source LLC
Chambersburg PA
CBHW080415060326
40689CB00019B/4255